GODS OF NORSE
(NORRøNE GUDER)

UMANG

Contents

Contents

Contents

THE CREATION OF THE WORLD — THE GIANTS — THE ÆSIR — MEN AND WOMEN — DWARFS — VANIR — ELVES

Our forefathers imagined the infinities of space to be a profound abyss, to which they gave the name *Ginnunga-gap*; on one of its confines there were icy frosts and mists; on the other, flame and heat. The frozen reaches were known as the Home of Fogs, or Niflheim; the torrid region as Muspellsheim, which may perhaps be rendered, the Home of Desolation. As the ice of Niflheim gradually melted away before the heat of Muspellsheim, there flowed forth from Niflheim into Ginnunga-gap chill streams of venom (the *Élivágar*), and yet the animating beams from Muspellsheim called the first living beings into life: a prodigious Giant (*jotunn*), called Ymir or Aurgelmir, and the cow Audhumla, from whose milk he drew sustenance. From Ymir in turn sprang other Giants, and thus he became the progenitor of all that evil race. The cow Audhumla likewise brought about life anew by licking the icebound boulders of salt. In this manner Buri came into being; his son Borr, with Bestla, daughter of the Giant Bolthorn, had three sons, named Odin, Vili, and Ve. These sons of Borr were good and fair to see; they became the forebears of the race of the Æsir.[1]

When the descendants of Ymir had multiplied beyond number, the sons of Borr put Ymir to death; in his blood all of the Giants were drowned except Bergelmir, who with his wife saved himself by means of a boat. The Æsir thus failed in their attempt to exterminate the race of Giants, and Bergelmir's kindred grew to a mighty host. The Giants, or Jotuns, were also known by the names Thursar (*pursar*), Rime-Thursar (*hrímpursar*), Ettins (*risar*), Cliff-Ettins (*bergrisar*), and Trolls (*troll*); they persisted in the most evil courses. From the body of Ymir the sons of Borr made earth, sky, and sea. The body itself became the earth, the bones became mountains and stones, the hair became trees and grass, the skull became the vault of heaven, the brain became clouds, and the maggots in Ymir's body became small Dwarfs, who dwelt beneath the earth's surface and in rocks, and who lived on a better footing with the Giants than with the Æsir.

Odin, Vili, and Ve, the sons of Borr, were at first the only Æsir. Not content with shaping inanimate nature, they brought to life sentient beings as well, both men and animals. The first human pair, Ask and Embla, they created from two trees. Odin gave them breath, Vili[1] gave them soul or understanding, and Ve (Lodur) gave them bodily warmth and color. From these two sprang the entire race of men.

The sons of Borr likewise created the celestial bodies. To this end they employed the sparks that flew into space out of Muspellsheim. The sun and the moon were placed each on its wain, and each wain was drawn by two horses; the horses of the sun were named Arvak and Alsvin.[1] Before the sun stands the shield Svalin.[2] As drivers of the wains were appointed the two beautiful children of Mundilfari, called Sun and Moon. Mundilfari was so proud of the two that he had named his daughter after the sun and his son after the moon; as a punishment the Æsir gave the children the task of guiding the wains of the sun and the moon. Moon once carried away from the earth two small children just as they left the well Byrgir carrying the cruse Sœg slung from their shoulders on a pole called Simul. The two children were named Bil and Hjuki, and their father's name was Vidfinn. Since that time they have followed the moon in his course.

The Giants or the Rime-Thursar continued without ceasing to disquiet the Æsir and disturb their labors. A hideous Giantess, mother of a great brood of Giant werewolves, bore among the others two called Skoll and Hati, who took up the pursuit of Sun and Moon, to devour them. Sun and Moon therefore must needs make haste in their journey across the heavens; yet in the end their pursuers will overtake them. Hati was the more forbidding of the two; he was known also as Manigarm, or the MoonHound. Toward the race of men the Giants were so ill-disposed that the Æsir found themselves compelled to build from the eyebrows of Ymir a great defensive fortress encompassing the midmost region of the earth. The fortress and all that it contained bore the name Midgard; beyond its confines lay Jotunheim. In the centre of the universe the Æsir established their own dwelling, Asgard; there Odin had his own seat, Lidskjalf, from which he might survey the whole universe, both the heavens and the earth, and see all that happened there. The race of the Æsir here grew to a goodly number; Odin particularly had many children.

Aside from the Æsir, the Dwarfs, and the Giants, our forefathers peopled the universe with other supernatural beings, such as the Vanir and the Elves. To the Vanir, dwelling in Vanaheim, the direction of the forces of nature seems particularly to have been attributed. Once upon a time, so the story runs, hostilities arose between the Æsir and the Vanir; the dispute ended with a treaty of peace, the terms of which prescribed an exchange of hostages. The Æsir delegated Hœnir; the Vanir delegated Njord, who in this way came to be numbered among the Æsir. The other deities who came from the Vanir were Frey and Freyja. Of the Elves, beings who associated preferably with men, some were good and some were evil. The good Elves, called Bright-Elves (*ljós-alfar*), who were brighter than the sun, had their abode in Alfheim; the evil Elves, called Dark-Elves (*svart-alfar, døkk-alfar*), were blacker than pitch, had their homes beneath the surface of the earth, and so are often confused with the Dwarfs.

CHAPTER TWO

THE PLAINS OF IDA — VALHALLA — YGGDRASIL

In Asgard the Æsir built an immense fortress, in the midst of which lay the Plains of Ida. Here they erected two splendid halls: Gladsheim, which contained high seats for Odin and the twelve peers among the Æsir; and Vingolf, which had high seats for Frigg and the goddesses. Round about Lidskjalf, whence Odin surveys the universe, rose the hall Valaskjalf, roofed with a silver roof.[1] The chief of the halls of Asgard, however, was Valhalla, the banquet hall of the Æsir. Here Odin held high festival not only for the Æsir, but for all the translated heroes (*einherjar*), brave warriors who after death came into his presence. In Valhalla there were 640 portals, through each of which, 960 warriors might march in abreast.

Between heaven and earth the Æsir constructed a bridge called Bifrost, or the Rainbow. The ruddy hue of the bridge is the light of a fire that burns without ceasing to prevent the Giants from crossing over it. Bifrost is of all bridges the most splendid and the strongest, and yet at last it will fall asunder, when the end of all things shall have come.

Besides Odin, there were twelve of the Æsir who were held to be chief deities of the universe; among themselves they had apportioned rule over all things, and each day they held counsel about what events should come to pass. Odin was their lord; he was supreme, mightiest of the gods, the preserver of all things, and therefore he was called All-Father. In Gladsheim, where stood the high seats of the gods, they took counsel together. As rulers of the universe the gods bore the titles *regin* or rogn, governors; bond or hopt, binding or uniting powers; and year, the holy ones. Their high seats were also called judgment seats (rokstólar). The gods or Æsir were designated as white, bright, shining, holy, mighty; as war-gods (*sigtívar*) or battle-gods (*valtívar*). They loved the race of men, protected men against Giants, Dwarfs, and Dark-Elves, and upheld righteousness and justice.

When the gods held their solemn assemblies, to which came all the Æsir, they resorted to the ash Yggdrasil, the tree of the universe. Here was their principal sanctuary. The ash Yggdrasil spread its branches abroad over the whole world. It had three roots: one among the Æsir, another among the Rime-Thursar, a third in the depths of Niflheim. Beside the root in Niflheim there was a fearsome well, Vergelmir; there lay a dreadful serpent, Nidhogg, which, together with a great number of other serpents, gnawed without respite at the root of the tree, threatening to destroy it. Beside the root that rested with the Rime-Thursar there was also a well, which belonged to a Giant, the wise Mimir; in it lay hidden the highest wisdom, and from it Mimir drank each day. Beside the third root, which stretched out to the Æsir, there was also a well, called

Urd's Well. It was here that the gods held their assembly. Among the branches of the ash many animals had their resort; there were a sagacious eagle, a hawk, four stags, and the little squirrel Ratatosk, which continually ran up and down bearing evil communications between the eagle and Nidhogg.

CHAPTER THREE

ODIN

Odin, the supreme deity, had, besides the title of All-Father, many other names. He was called Ygg (The Awful), Gagnrad (He Who Determines Victories), Herjan (God of Battles), Har (The High One), Jafnhar (Even as High), Thridi (Third),[1] Nikar, Nikud, Bileyg (One With Evasive Eyes), Baleyg (One With Flaming Eyes), Bolverk (The Worker of Misfortune), Sigfather (The Father of Battle or of Victory), Gaut (The Creator or, the "Geat"), Roptatyr, Valfather (Father of the Slain),[2] etc. Odin was the wisest of all the gods; from him the others always sought counsel when need arose. He drew wisdom from the well of the Giant Mimir. Having placed one of his eyes in pawn with Mimir, Odin invariably appeared as a one-eyed, rather oldish man;[3] otherwise he 'was represented as strong and well-favored, and as armed with spear and shield. In Valhalla and Vingolf, where Odin gave banquets to gods and heroes, he himself partook of nothing but wine, which to him was both meat and drink; the meat that was placed before him he gave to his two wolves, Geri and Freki.[4] Odin also had two ravens, Hugin and Munin (Thought and Memory), which perched one on each of his shoulders. To them he owed a great part of his wisdom; every day they flew forth through the expanses of the universe, returning at supper to tell him all that they had seen; therefore Odin was called also the God of Ravens. From his high seat, Lidskjalf in Valaskjalf, Odin saw all that came to pass. On his horse, Sleipnir, which was eight-footed and the fleetest horse in the world, he rode wherever he wished. His spear Gungnir would strike whatsoever he aimed at. On his arm he wore the precious ring Draupnir; from it dropped every ninth night eight other rings as splendid as itself.

The worship of Odin appears to have consisted in part in a peculiar kind of human sacrifice, and this circumstance had much to do with our forefathers' regarding him as a stern and cruel deity. Just as Odin himself hung upon a gallows, wounded with the thrust of a spear, and devoted to himself,[1] so, according to certain legendary narratives[2] it was a custom to dedicate men to Odin by hanging them on a gallows and piercing them with spears. The skalds thus referred to Odin as the "God of Hanged Men" or the "Lord of the Gallows." He bade his raven fly to such as had been hanged, or he went in person to the gallows tree and by means of incantations compelled the hanged man to hold discourse with him. An historian of the eleventh century, Adam of Bremen, recounts that in the sacrificial grove near the temple at Uppsala many human bodies hung from the branches of the sacred trees.[1] This record no doubt has to do with sacrifices to Odin. With these very sacrifices to Odin what Snorri relates in the *Ynglinga Saga* must be closely connected; as the story reads there, Odin immediately before his death caused his body to be marked with the point of a spear, and "dedicated to himself all men who died by force of arms"; "Njord died of disease, but he let himself be marked for dedication to Odin before he died." Thus it was possible for Odin to accept human sacrifice not only by means of hanging but through a ceremonial procedure by which one who wished to avoid dying a natural death made an incision on his body with a spear. And one who advanced to meet an opposing army might, before joining battle, devote the enemy to Odin by hurling a spear over the heads of the hostile force, with the words, "Odin possesses you all." Odin took pleasure in such a sacrifice; to him it was a matter of great moment to surround himself with as many Heroes as possible in preparation for the ultimate warfare against the enemies of gods'and men.

Among the Æsir there were several gods of war, but Odin was foremost. From him battle took the name of "Odin's Tempest" and "Ygg's Game"; and the spear, "Odin's Fire." The worship of Odin as the supreme deity was not, however, universally prevalent; the cult bound up with his name seems to have come from the South into the North at a comparatively late date. Place names in which the name of Odin forms a compounding element provide valuable aid in determining the limits of Odin worship in various regions.[1]

Jord and Frigg were the wives of Odin; his concubines, the Giantess Grid, and Rind; his sons were Thor (with Jord), Balder (with Frigg), Vidar (with Grid), Vali (with Rind), and besides, Heimdal, Hod, and Bragi; all these were numbered among the chief deities. Other sons are Tyr, Meili, and Hermod, the messenger sent by the gods to Hell upon the death of Balder. Ancient kings and princes were proud to count their descent from Odin; for this reason other sons were later attributed to him, such as Skjold, ancestor of the kings of Denmark, Sæming, ancestor of the Haloigja family (the earls of Lade), Sigi, ancestor of the Volsungs, and still others.

CHAPTER FOUR

THOR

Next after Odin, the principal deity was Thor. He it was who guarded men and their labors from the wild forces of nature, personified as Giants. Thus he held sway — in certain Northern regions — over air and climate, over rain and harvest.[2] As the god of fertility, however, he had to divide his rule with the gods of the Vanir; but thunder and lightning always were the special province of Thor, who according to the Norse myths was constantly engaged in battle against the Giants. He rode in a chariot which, as it rolled along, produced thunder.[1] The chariot was drawn by two goats, Tanngnjost[2] and Tanngrisni;[3] these goats Thor could kill and eat and bring to life once more provided all the bones are gathered up in the hides. Because Thor usually drove these goats, he was called Riding-Thor;[4] he had other names as well, such as Ving-Thor, Lorridi, Einridi.

Thor's realm was known as Thrudvang; there stood his imposing hall, Bilskirnir, the largest in the world, comprising 540 rooms. To Thor belonged three objects of price: the most valuable of these was the hammer Mjollnir, which he carried whenever he gave battle to the Giants; he could make it as great or as small as he pleased, he could hurl it, through the air, and it always found its mark and returned of itself to his hand. Again, he had remarkable iron gauntlets with which to grasp the hammer; and he had a belt of strength which, when he girdled it about him, added to his Æsir power. Without Thor the Æsir would have found no help against the Giants; but no sooner did they mention him by name than he gave proof of his prowess. He was wedded to beautiful Sif, of the golden hair;[5] their children were Modi and a daughter named Thrud. With the Giantess Jarnsaxa he had besides a son called Magni.

Thor was hot and hasty of temper; when he rode out to meet the Giants, the mountains trembled and the earth burst into flame. When the gods repaired to Yggdrasil to hold assembly there, Thor did not trouble himself to cross by way of Bifrost but took a shorter road on which he waded the deepest streams. Now and then he might chance to leap before he looked; and so once or twice he came out of some enterprise or other with harm and confusion.[1]

The worship of Thor was very widespread throughout the North. Numerous place names bear witness to his cult,[2] and the sagas contain not infrequent accounts of sanctuaries dedicated to Thor or of invocations directed to him.[3] To our ancestors Thor was tall and strong, handsome and dignified; he had a red beard, and gripped Mjollnir in his hand.

CHAPTER FIVE

BALDER

The son of Odin and Frigg is Balder, the god of innocence and piety. He is so bright and fair that light shines from his features; he is also wise, eloquent, gentle, and lenient, and righteous to such a degree that his judgments stand always unshaken. His home and stronghold is called Breidablik;[4] there nothing impure may find lodgment. His wife is the faithful Nanna, daughter of Nep. His son is the righteous Forseti. Balder was killed by his brother Hod, but after the destruction of the universe he will return again.[1]

The cult of Balder is mentioned only in the late, unhistorical *Fridthjof's Saga*; from this source we learn that he had a great sanctuary,

Baldershagi, somewhere in Sogn.

CHAPTER SIX

NJORD

Njord (*Njorðr*, originally *Nerpuz*) guides the course of the winds and governs sea and fire; he grants to those who call upon him good fortune at sea and in the chase, and he dispenses wealth, whether of lands or of chattels. Of old he came from Vanaheim.[3] It so befell that when the Æsir and the Vanir were engaged in concluding a treaty of peace, each race gave hostages to the other, the Æsir designating Hœnir and the Vanir, Njord; they all spat in a crock, and from the spittle they made a man, the sapient Kvasir. From that time forth Njord was reckoned among the Æsir and took rank with the foremost of them. His dwelling, called Noatun, is near the sea; outside the walls swim swans and water fowl of all sorts. Njord's children are the god Frey and the goddess Freyja; his wife, their stepmother, is Skadi, a Giantess. The Æsir having brought about the death of her father Thjazi,[4] Skadi went in arms to Asgard to demand recompense. In order to pacify her, the Æsir permitted her to choose a husband from their number, but she was to see only their feet and to make her choice in this way. She fixed her eyes on a pair of shapely feet and, supposing them to be Balder's, chose accordingly. But her choice fell on Njord, with whom she did not live on the very best of terms; Skadi wished to make her abode in Thrymheim, her old home, but Njord wished to remain in Noatun. So they agreed to live by turns nine nights in Thrymheim and three nights in Noatun. When they had stayed the first nine nights in Thrymheim, Njord said that he was utterly weary of the mountains; the howling of the wolves seemed to him most lugubrious as compared with the singing of the swans. Skadi found herself disappointed likewise; when she had remained three nights in Noatun, she was no less weary of the screaming of the birds and the roaring of the sea, which broke her repose. Thus perforce they went their own ways; Skadi returned to Thrymheim, where she disported herself in skiing and hunting and so earned the sobriquet of the Ski-Deity or the Ski-Goddess (ondurdís).

Njord was called the Scion of the Vanir, the Vanir-God, the God Without Blemish. According to the testimony of place names,[1] his cult was widespread throughout the North. At the ancient sacrificial feasts, men drank to Njord and Frey next after Odin;[2] and from an early formulary for taking oaths it is manifest that oaths were sworn by Njord and Frey and by the "almighty god" (presumably Thor).

CHAPTER SEVEN

FREY

Njord's son is Frey, who is fair to look upon, mightier and more valorous than even his own father. He governs weather and tillage; in his hand lie prosperity, joy, and peace. Like Njord, Frey is called Scion of the Vanir, the Vanir-God; also, God of the Seasons and Giver of Riches. He holds sway over Alfheim and the Bright-Elves.

Frey has certain priceless talismans that cunning Dwarfs have made for him. First of these is the ship Skidbladnir, which sails over land and sea alike; when its sails are hoisted the winds always favor its course, and it is so devised that it can be folded together and kept in a pocket till the time for its use has come. He has also a marvelous boar, named Gullinbusti or Slidrugtanni, that races through the air and over the sea, throwing beams of light from his golden bristles; Frey often hitches the boar to his chariot when he wishes to drive abroad. Frey is wedded to Gerd, fair daughter of the Giant Gymir. Her he caught sight of one day as he had taken his seat in Lidskjalf to gaze out upon all the worlds; far to the north he saw her walking across her father's farmyard; air and sea shone with brightness as she raised her white arm to close the door. Frey fell in love with her, and for sorrow could neither sleep nor drink.

His father Njord sent Skirnir, Frey's servant, to learn what was amiss with him; then Frey confessed his longing and commanded Skirnir to run his errand and pay court on his behalf.

Skirnir promised to go if Frey would only lend him his magic sword, whose blade, if need be, could strike of its own power. Thus armed he went forth on his quest; and through sorcery he constrained Gerd to promise a meeting with Frey; the appointed tryst was to take place after the lapse of nine nights, and in the interval Frey was beside himself with longing. Frey afterward missed his trusty sword; in a duel with the Giant Beli he was compelled to use the antlers of a stag to kill his opponent. When the end of the world comes, he will feel still more keenly the want of his sword. Snorri relates that his violent love for Gerd was a penalty laid upon him by Odin because Frey had ventured to sit in Odin's seat.

The worship of Frey was general throughout the North, and place names demonstrate that many sanctuaries were dedicated to him.[1] The Swedes showed particular zeal in the cult of Frey; and from Yngvi-Frey (*Yngvi*, *Yngvifreyr*, also Ing or *Ingunar-freyr*) in Uppsala, the family of the Ynglings, Norway's royal house, is said to have descended. There are accounts of horses dedicated to Frey, the so-called Manes of Frey. In Sweden a priestess of his cult was given to Frey for a wife, with whom he is supposed to have lived in actual marriage.

CHAPTER EIGHT

TYR

Tyr, Odin's son with the daughter of the Giant Hymir, is bold and courageous; men call upon him in battle, and he gives them courage and heroism. Therefore Tyr is the true god of war; he takes pleasure in bringing about strife, and he does nothing whatever for the promotion of concord. Captains and princes are designated after him, Kinsmen of Tyr. No small number of places in the North (mostly in Denmark) commemorate his name; and yet, few traditions connected with him have survived. He has but one hand; the other was bitten off by the Fenris Wolf.

CHAPTER NINE

HEIMDAL

Heimdal is another of the chief gods; according to report he was considered great and holy, and bore the appellation of the White God. He was born in a miraculous manner of nine Giant maidens, on the confines of the earth, in the morning of time; and he drew his sustenance from the earth. By some he was called Odin's son. His teeth are of gold; by night or day his vision spans a hundred miles of space; he is able to hear the growing of grass upon the ground and of wool on the backs of sheep; therefore he is a fit watchman for the gods. He dwells near Bifrost, which he guards against the Giants. He has an immense horn, the Gjallar-Horn; when he blows it, the sound is heard in all the worlds. His dwelling at the brink of heaven is known as the Mount of Heaven (*Himinbjorg*). For the rest, report has little to say of Heimdal. He is also called Gullintanni, by reason of his golden teeth; another of his names is Hallinskidi.

The skalds make frequent mention of him; gold they refer to as "Heimdal's Teeth," and to his sword they give the designation "*hofuð* (*manns*)," i.e., "(man's) head," in allusion to an obscure myth. His horse bears the name of Goldtop.

CHAPTER TEN

BRAGI

Bragi, son of Odin, is the god of eloquence and the art of poetry. Our forefathers thought of him as a venerable man with a long beard. After him, according to Snorri, all manner of minstrelsy is given the title *bragr*. Idun is his wife; to her belong the marvelous apples which restore youth to the gods when old age comes upon them.

CHAPTER ELEVEN

FORSETI

Forseti, the son of Balder and Nanna, is the god of justice and conciliation. Those who refer their disputes to him never go away unreconciled. The hall where he sits in judgment is known as Glitnir; its pillars are of gold and its roof is of silver. Forseti must have had no small number of worshippers; a reminiscence of the cult is to be found in a Norwegian place name, Forsetelund in Onsøy, Østfold.

CHAPTER TWELVE

HOD — VALI — VIDAR — ULL

Concerning the four major gods Hod, Vali, Vidar, and Ull, few references are found in Norse sources. Hod, the son of Odin, is blind but vigorous; he it is who unwittingly brings about the death of Balder; he is subsequently killed by Vali and he will not return until after the universe has come to destruction. Vali (also called by Snorri, less correctly, Ali) is the son of Odin and Rind. He has his own house in Valaskjalf,[1] and is a bold warrior and a good archer. He will neither wash himself nor clip his hair until he has taken vengeance upon Hod for the death of Balder, and he will survive the destruction of the universe. Vidar too shall return after Ragnarok. He is the son of Odin and the Giantess Grid, and next to Thor he is the strongest of the gods. He is called The God of Few Words. When Ragnarok, the Twilight of the Gods, is come, he will avenge Odin by cleaving with his thick boot the throat of the Fenris Wolf. His dwelling is in Vidi. Ull is fair to look upon, a mighty bowman and ski-runner; men do well to summon him to their aid in single combat. He is the son of Sif and the stepson of Thor. His dwelling bears the name of Ydalir.

CHAPTER THIRTEEN

HŒNIR – LODUR

Hœenir and Lodur are also reckoned, though very infrequently, among the gods. Hœnir's name is found in the Prose Edda among the major divinities, and he appears besides as the companion of Odin. According to the Voluspá, Lodur takes part with Odin and Hœnir in the creation of man. These three "mighty and benevolent Æsir" once came down to the seashore, where they found Ask and Embla lying lifeless, without breath, without soul, and without blood; Odin gave them breath, Hœnir gave them soul, and Lodur gave them blood and bodily color. According to the *Prose Edda*, however, it was the sons of Borr, namely Odin, Vili, and Ve, who created Ask and Embla. Odin, Hœnir, and Lodur, or Odin, Vili, and Ve thus function as a sort of trinity of the Æsir. In the *Gylfaginning* something of the kind is to be found in Snorri's formulation of the ancient mythology, namely, the trinity *Hár* (The High), *Jafnhár* (The Equally High), and *priði* (The Third). At the end of the war between the Æsir and the Vanir, Hœnir was delivered over to the Vanir as a hostage.[1] As the more complete account runs in Snorri's *Ynglinga Saga*: Hœnir was a tall and handsome man, whom the Æsir declared to be well fitted to be made a chieftain;

but for fuller security they sent the wise Mimir with him. Hœnir was at once given leadership in Vanaheim, and all went well so long as Mimir remained at his side; but when Hœnir, in the absence of Mimir, had to make difficult decisions, he invariably declared that "others must determine that." Whereupon the Vanir at length lost patience, killed Mimir, and sent his head back to the Æsir. On the evidence of Snorri's *Edda*, Hœnir was also called The Fleet God or The Long-Footed God or The King of Eld (*aurkonungr*, Snorri's *Edda* I, 168). In the "Saga Fragment" mentioned below,[2] Rœrek Slœngvandbaugi — brother of king Helgi and son-in-law of Ivar Vidfadmir — is compared with Hœnir, who here is called the most timorous of the Æsir. Possibly other myths having to do with him have failed to survive.

CHAPTER FOURTEEN

LOKI AND HIS CHILDREN

The twelve major deities in the mythology of the *Eddas* were, as already, enumerated, — in addition to Odin — Thor, Njord, Frey, Balder, Tyr, Heimdal, Bragi, Forseti, Hod, Vidar, Vali, and Ull. Next after these is mentioned, among the foremost Æsir, Loki or Lopt, although he is more properly to be counted their enemy. By race he was a Giant, his father being the Giant Farbauti and his mother the Giantess Laufey or Nal; yet he became the foster brother of Odin and was numbered among the Æsir. His brothers were Byleist (also called Byleipt) and Helblindi. Loki was wellfavored, but crafty and malicious. To be sure, he was sometimes compelled to make good the evil he had done, and occasionally he even placed his cunning at the service of the Æsir in seasons of great need; yet in all that really mattered he remained their enemy and the secret friend of the Giants. Loki was the actual instigator of the death of Balder. At the last day he will reappear as one of the captains of the Giants, and his terrible progeny will cause much more harm than even he himself. With the Giantess Angerboda in Jotunheim he had three children:

Fenrir, Jormungand, and Hel. Fenrir was a ravening wolf, known also as the Fenris Wolf; Jormungand was a hideous, venom-spewing serpent; and Hel was a horrible hag. These three were fostered as children in Jotunheim, and the gods foreknew that Loki's offspring would work them great evil. Therefore the All-Father, Odin, commanded them to be brought before him. The gods forebore to put them to death, for the course of fate was not to be broken, neither was the sacred refuge of Valhalla to be contaminated; so the gods sought other means of being rid of the three. Hel they thrust into the depths of Niflheim to hold sway there and to receive in her abode all who should die of illness or old age, whether men or other beings of earth. Jormungand they hurled into the deep sea of the universe, where he grew and waxed so great as to be able to encompass the earth and to bite his own tail. Therefore he is commonly called the Midgard Serpent, since he holds all of Midgard encircled. The Wolf, on the other hand, was nurtured in Asgard and was so ferocious that none but Tyr dared to bring him food. When the gods saw that he was growing altogether too rapidly, they became much alarmed and undertook to bind him fast. They declared that they desired, just in sport, to try his strength by testing his ability to break a chain which they had provided for the purpose. The Wolf, falling in with their wishes, consented to be bound but at once burst his fetters. He did likewise with a second chain, twice as strong as the first. Then the All-Father sent Skirnir on an errand to certain Dwarfs living in the home of the Dark Elves, to have them forge a chain that the Wolf should not be able to break asunder. The Dwarfs accordingly made a chain from the sound of a cat's footfall, the beard of a woman, the roots of a mountain, the sinews of a bear, the breath of fishes, and the spittle of birds; this is the reason why the footfall of the cat no longer has any sound, why women have no beards, why mountains have no roots, and so on. The chain, called Gleipnir, was fine and soft as silk. The Æsir led the Wolf out upon the island of Lyngvi in the lake named Amsvartnir and there asked him if he would submit to being bound with Gleipnir. The Wolf, suspecting some trick, gave his consent only on the condition that one of them would place a hand in his mouth as an earnest of his release if the chain should remain unbroken. The Æsir, unwilling to take such a risk, looked doubtfully at one another; finally Tyr stepped forward and laid his hand in the Wolf's muzzle. The Wolf was then bound. The more he struggled to free himself, the tighter held the chain; by no means was he able to break it and, since the Æsir had no thought of letting him go, he bit off Tyr's hand. The Æsir drew the end of the chain through a great slab of rock, thrust it deep into the ground, and laid a huge boulder over it. The Wolf, mad with rage, snapped and bit at everything round about; but they thrust a sword into his mouth so that his jaws gaped wide. He howls dismally, and slaver runs from him like a river. Thus he shall lie bound till the world comes to an end; but then he will gain his freedom, will prove to be the worst enemy of the gods, and will even swallow up Odin himself. But the Wolf will be killed by Vidar.

In regard to all the malicious tricks Loki played on the Æsir and the punishments he suffered in consequence, further accounts will follow. His wife was Sigyn, with whom he had several sons. Besides, he became in a peculiar manner the father, or rather the mother, of Odin's horse Sleipnir. It happened in this way. When Midgard had been created and the gods were meditating the building of a massive stronghold as a bulwark against the Giants, a Giant smith came forward and offered to build the stronghold in a year's time if he might have Freyja, the sun, and the moon by way of payment; but if on the first day of summer any part of the work remained undone, he was to receive no wages. The Æsir felt secure in making such a promise, and crafty Loki urged them on. But the building proceeded more rapidly than they had thought possible; for the Giant's powerful horse, Svadilfari, during the night pulled into place stones as huge as mountains. When only three days remained before summertide, the Giant was already busied with the castle gate, and the Æsir were growing uneasy; at no price whatever were they prepared to surrender Freyja, the sun, and the moon. They commanded into their presence Loki, whose bad counsel was the cause of their trouble, threatened him with death, and thus frightened him into promising to find a way out of their difficulties. Transforming himself into a mare, he ran whinnying out from the forest at evening just as

Svadilfari was at his task of hauling stone. Svadilfari broke loose and followed the mare into the woods, pursued in turn by the builder; that whole night not a stone was hauled, and thus the work was interrupted. The mason was enraged; but Thor crushed his head with Mjollnir. The mare — or Loki — later foaled Sleipnir, the world's fleetest horse, a gray with eight feet.

CHAPTER FIFTEEN

HERMOD — SKIRNIR

Among various subordinate Æsir, who in their own right are powerful enough, but who virtually serve as retainers to the others, appear Hermod and Skirnir. Skirnir, Frey's servant, has already been discussed.[1] Hermod is the son of Odin, and bears the sobriquet, "the resolute"; he is employed in all sorts of errands and embassies. Odin himself presented his son with helmet and byrnie. Hermod is celebrated for his mission to Hel for the purpose of bringing Balder back again. It is Hermod and Bragi who go forth to meet Hakon the Good and to bid him welcome to Valhalla on Odin's behalf.

CHAPTER SIXTEEN

THE GODDESSES — FRIGG — JORD — FREYJA

Among the goddesses there are likewise, besides Odin's wife Frigg, twelve or thirteen of the highest rank, namely: Freyja, Saga, Eir, Gefjon, Sjofn, Lofn, Var, Vor, Syn, Lin, Snotra, Fulla, and Gna; all of these are enumerated together in Snorri's Edda. Fulla and Gna, and to a certain degree Lin as well, are merely handmaidens of Frigg; in their stead may therefore be placed Idun, Nanna, and Sif, all of whom are far more important. Next in order come Sigyn, Gerd, and Skadi, who however are of Giant race; and thereafter some of the daughters of the gods and the goddesses. Jord and Rind are also counted among the goddesses.

Frigg is the daughter of Fjorgynn;[1] she is the wife of Odin, the mother of Balder, and chief among the goddesses. Her house is the splendid Fensalir. The goddesses Lin, Fulla, and Gna are closely associated with her. Lin is set to guard those of mankind whom Frigg desires to preserve from harm. Fulla, a maiden with long flowing hair and a golden chaplet about her brow, carries Frigg's hand casket, keeps watch and ward over her shoes, and shares her secrets. Gna runs errands for Frigg through the various worlds, especially in matters requiring despatch, in which instances she rides the horse Hofvarpnir, who races through the air and over the waters. Something is to be learned of the cult of Frigg by means of Norwegian and Swedish place names,[2] and her name occurs also among German and English tribes.[3] The Frigg of the *Eddas* was no doubt derived from an ancient goddess of earth or of fertility, according to the testimony of both her own name and her father's.[4] Further evidence is to be discovered in the manifest connection between Frigg, daughter of Fjorgynn, and Jord, Thor's mother, who bears the additional name Fjorgyn.

Freyja, of the race of the Vanir, is a daughter of Njord and a sister of Frey. As the story reads she was, at the treaty of peace with the Vanir, delivered over by them and-accepted by the Æsir among the goddesses. She was wedded to Od, but he left her and went out into foreign lands; she often wept over him, wept golden tears. Her daughters, Noss and Gersemi, were so beautiful that from them all precious gems have taken their names; and from Freyja the designation *freyja* or *frúva*[1] is likewise said to have been formed. Freyja was in the habit of driving a cart drawn by two cats; and she had in her possession the magnificent necklace called Brisingamen.[2] She dwelt in Folkvang, in the great hall named Sessrymnir. Of all the heroes who fell in battle, half became her portion; it was her right to choose them, and to her they came in Folkvang. She had special authority in the relations of love, yet she was not the only goddess of love to whom men had recourse; Sjofn had the power to kindle love between men and women, and Lofn to help those who loved each other but who met with difficulties in winning the beloved.

Freyja had several names. She was called Vanadis because she came of the race of the Vanir. At one time she set out in search of Od, on which occasion she adopted various names, as follows: Mardol, Horn (or Hœrn?), Gefn, and Syr.

CHAPTER SEVENTEEN

SAGA — EIR — GEFJON — VAR — VOR — SYNSNOTRA

In the array of goddesses in the Prose *Edda*, Saga is found next after Frigg; possibly Saga is only another name for Frigg. Her house is known as Sœkkvabek;[1] cool waves wash over her dwelling, and here Odin and she drink each day from crocks of gold. Some generations since, it was a common opinion that she was the goddess of history, "saga"; but it is certain that her name was *Sága* and not *Saga* (with a short vowel). No more reasonable explanation has been proposed than that the name may have been formed from a root found in at *sjá* (Gothic *saihwan*) and thus has the meaning: she who sees — and knows — all things, in common with Odin.[2] Eir is the goddess of healing, her name having originally been the common noun *eir*, "mercy." Gefjon, according to Snorri's *Edda*, was a maiden, to whom came after death all who died maids. Odin says of her in *Lokasenna* that she knows the fates as well as himself. It thus seems as if Gefjon, like Saga, corresponds to Odin's wife Frigg. There is another myth having to do with a Gefjon who was one of Odin's following. She asked king Gylfi of Sweden for as much land as she could plow around in one day, and he promised her the gift. She accordingly transformed her sons into oxen, put them before the plow, and with them she plowed loose all the land that once lay where now lies Lake Mälaren. This parcel of earth she drew out into the Baltic, and the land is now called Zealand; there she made her home, and there she was wedded to Odin's son Scyld. Var[1] hears the oaths of fidelity that men and women make to each other. Hence, if report be true, these promises are known as *várar*, and Var punishes those who break them. Vor[2] is endowed with prudence; she searches into all things so that nothing remains hidden from her. Syn "guards the door of the hall" and prevents the unworthy from entering; she also hinders men from bearing false witness in courts of law; thence, says Snorri, we get *syn*, "the act of denying" (*at synja*). Snotra is wise and decorous of manner.

CHAPTER EIGHTEEN

IDUN — NANNA — SIF

Little is known of Idun, Nanna, and Sif. Idun, the wife of Bragi, had in her possession the most priceless treasures of the Æsir, certain apples that restored youth to those who ate of them. Without them the Æsir would have become old and feeble. For this reason they were fearful of losing Idun, so that on one occasion when she had been carried off by the Giant Thjazi[4] they were in the most dire straits. Idun was designated as the "Goddess of Brunnaker's Bench," presumably the name of the dwelling where she and Bragi were housed. Nanna, daughter of Nep, was the wife of Balder, whom she so loved that her heart broke at his death. Sif was the wife of Thor. She had been wedded before, to whom we do not know; and she was the mother of Ull, who is called the stepson of Thor. Sif was fair and had gold hair fashioned for her by cunning Dwarfs. Her name, meaning "kindred," "relationship," indicates that she was thought of as the protector of homes, just as Thor was the protector of Midgard.[1] Sigyn, Skadi, and Gerd have already been discussed.

CHAPTER NINETEEN

THE NORNS

Next in order to the major gods and goddesses were other powerful divinities, and besides, certain supernatural beings of a lower degree. Most highly regarded were probably the Norns, the goddesses of Destiny. Though their number was rather large, three of them were more prominent than the rest, namely, Urd, Verdandi, and Skuld, who dwelt beneath Yggdrasil, beside the well which after Urd is called Urd's Well, where two swans resort, where the branches of Yggdrasil drip honey dew, and where the gods meet in solemn assembly. The Norns control the destiny of all men and even of the Æsir themselves; and they direct the immutable laws of the universe. At the birth of every child the Norns are present to determine its fate, and no man lives one day longer than the Norns grant him leave. There are both good

CHAPTER TWENTY

FAMILIAR SPIRITS — ATTENDANT SPIRITS

Related to the Norns were the Familiar Spirits (*hamingjur*) and the Attendant Spirits (*fylgjur*). The Familiar Spirits were supernatural, usually invisible feminine beings who accompanied men and directed their course. Each person had his Familiar Spirit, who strove to bring him good luck;[1] it was possible to lend one's Familiar Spirit to another in case one desired to run a risk in his behalf. The Attendant Spirits (*fylgjur*), on the other hand, ordinarily had the shape of animals who walked before men or beside them. Each person had, according to the belief of our fathers, one or more Attendant Spirits; and certain people pretended that they could see the Attendant Spirits and thus ascertain in advance who was drawing near. The Attendant Spirit usually corresponded to the character of the individual in question; powerful chieftains had bears, bulls, and the like as Attendant Spirits, crafty folk had foxes, and so forth. Supernatural beings of this type were not made the object of worship or prayer. Tales have come down to us of sundry men to whom these beings by preference revealed themselves and who by such means gained an uncommon insight into the destinies of other men. Faith in Familiar Spirits and Attendant Spirits persisted after the introduction of Christianity; even zealous Christians like Olaf Tryggvason and Saint Olaf were not wholly free from such beliefs. Occasionally both of these classes of tutelary powers were designated outright as Norns; the popular mind appears not to have drawn a sharp distinction in this respect.

CHAPTER TWENTY-ONE

THE VALKYRIES

Other feminine beings who exercised control over the fates of men and were closely related to the Norns, were the Valkyries. Victory lay in their government, and mortality in battle; Odin sent them forth to "choose the slain" or the heroes who were doomed to fall.[1] They were therefore also called the Maidens of Odin. They were beautiful young girls; armed and fully panoplied, they rode through the air and over the waters, to the ends of the world. At home in Valhalla they served as cupbearers to the Æsir and Heroes in the halls of Odin. There were two classes of Valkyries: an original order, the celestial Valkyries; and another order, half mortal and half divine, who lived for a time among men as mortals but who later came to Odin in Valhalla, evidently a sort of feminine counterpart to the Heroes. The number of the celestial Valkyries is variously computed, as nine or as nine times nine; they were frequently imagined as riding about in three groups. Those most commonly mentioned were Gondul, Skogul (also called Geir-Skogul, or Spear-Skogul), Lokk, Rist, Mist, Hild, and others. Skuld[1] was also counted among the Valkyries. Besides these, there were other Valkyries who created dissension among the Heroes and who were employed only in the most menial tasks.

Valkyries, Norns, Familiar Spirits, Attendant Spirits, and occasionally even certain of the goddesses, notably Freyja,[2] were known by the general designation of Disir. Dís (plural *dísir*) was no doubt originally a term used to denote a distinct group of gods.[3] Worship of them consisted of a special kind of sacrifice (*dísablót*), doubtless a more intimate cult, participated in only by women; the Disir were supposed to have particular concern for the good of the home and the family, and in so far were not noticeably different from the Attendant Spirits of a family (*kynfylgjur, spádísir*), which have been discussed above.[4] From their number, however, proceeded a goddess who was to become the centre of a more general cult; and it must have been this goddess — perhaps *Vanadís*, Freyja — who was worshipped in Disarsal near Uppsala.[5] In connection with the annual sacrifice to the Disir at Uppsala were held also a court assembly (*dísaþing*) and a market; until very recent times the market-fair of Uppsala at Candlemass, early in February, was commonly called "Distingen," that is, the Disir court.

CHAPTER TWENTY-TWO

THORGERD HŒLGABRUD AND IRPA

Within one of the greater families, the ancestral Disir might attain the rank of goddesses and become the objects of something more than private worship. Of this there is an example in the goddesses of the Haloigja family, namely Thorgerd Hœlgabrud and her sister Irpa. Thorgerd was the daughter of an ancient mythical king Hœlgi, after whom Halogaland is said to have its name; that is, Hœlgi is the eponymous hero of the district, the personal name having been formed by the operation of myth to explain the place name. Thorgerd Hœlgabrud is also called, but less correctly, Horgabrud[1] and Horgatroll. In more recent saga tradition this designation of "troll" no doubt had some connection with the aid she was supposed to have given to Hakon, Earl of Lade, in the battle of Hjorungavag. According to Snorri's *Edda* (I, 400), her father also was worshipped; the mound in which he was buried was constructed from alternate layers of earth and stone, and of silver and gold — "these were the treasures offered up before him."

CHAPTER TWENTY-THREE

THE FORCES OF NATURE — ÆGIR

While the Æsir as major deities governed all the forces of Nature and strove to direct them in the interest of mankind, almost every natural force or element had its own indwelling divinity; this divinity, a kind of personification of the natural force or element itself, was able to set those forces in motion but unable to determine their activities wholly. Thus Njord governed the winds and guided their course, but he was not their prime mover; that function was fulfilled by the Giant Ræsvelg (*Hræsvelgr*, that is, Consumer of Corpses) who, sitting in the guise of an eagle at the northern confines of the heavens, produced the winds by the beating of his wings. So long as the rude powers of Nature are left to themselves, their activities are rather harmful than beneficent, for which reason it is no wonder that our fathers commonly regarded these elementary divinities as Giants; for it was distinctly characteristic of the Giants that they were seldom on good terms with the Æsir and that they constantly had to be kept in subjection. The most powerful of these lesser divinities were Fornjot and his kin. Fornjot, according to story, had three sons: Ler, Logi, and Kari. Ler ruled the sea, Logi ruled the fire, and Kari ruled the wind. Kari's son was named Jokul or Frosti; Frosti's son was named Snjo; and Snjo in turn had four children: Thorri, Fonn, Drifa, and Mjoll. Fornjot was no doubt originally a name for Giant;[1] he was probably to be identified with the primordial Giant Ymir. Kari means literally "wind,"[2] and Logi means "flame." Jokul means "icicle"; Frosti, "frost"; Snjo, "snow"; Thorri, "black frost"; Fonn, "perennial snowbank"; Drifa, "snowdrift"; Mjoll, "fine driving snow." The names themselves thus indicate what these divinities represented. Most remarkable of them all was Ler, god of the sea. He was also, indeed usually, called Ægir; and by reason of the similarity in names, Snorri fixes his abode on the island of Læsø in the Kattegat. At first he was no friend of the Æsir. Thor, however, intimidating him with piercing eyes, constrained him to give a banquet for the gods each winter in his own hall; later he in turn paid visits to the Æsir, who received him in a friendly manner. His banquets were in very truth merrymakings, at which ale flowed of its own accord; his hall was lighted by gleaming gold instead of candles; his brisk serving men, Eldir and Fimafeng, ministered to the guests. Yet now and again Ægir's evil nature got the upper hand. He kept meditating vengeance against Thor, who had presumed to lay commands upon him; at length he hit upon the plan of having Thor find for him a kettle large enough to brew ale for all the Æsir together. Such a kettle he knew was to be had from the Giant Hymir alone, and it was only after running many a risk that Thor succeeded in obtaining the kettle and carrying it away with him.[1] Ægir's wife, Ran, endeavored by all possible means to bring mischance upon mankind; she had in her possession a net, with which she made it her constant pursuit to draw seafaring men down to herself in the deeps of the ocean. Ægir and Ran had nine daughters; their names form various designations for the waves, which explains why the skalds sometimes describe the waves as Daughters of Ægir or of Ran. In the kenning for gold, "Ægir's Fire," the name of the god of the sea also occurs; gold, it will be remembered, was employed in the lighting of his banquet hall.

CHAPTER TWENTY-FOUR

NIGHT — DAY

The divinities of day and of night were also of Giant race. The Giant Norvi had a daughter by the name of Nott (Night), who was dark and swarthy like the rest of her kindred. She was first wedded to Naglfari, with whom she had a son named Aud; later, to Anar, with whom she had a daughter named Jord, who became the wife of Odin;[1] and finally, to Delling, of the race of the Æsir, with whom she had a son named Dag (Day), who was bright and fair like his father's family. The All-Father took Night and her son Day, gave them two horses and two wains, and stationed them aloft in the heavens, where they were to ride around the earth in alternating courses of twelve hours each. Night drives the horse known as Rimfaxi (*Hrímfaxi*, that is, "having a mane of rime"), and each morning the fields are bedewed with froth that drips from his bit. This horse is also called Fjorsvartnir (from *fjor*, "life," and *svartr*, "black"). Day drives Skinfaxi ("with the shining mane"); earth and sky sparkle with the light from his mane.

CHAPTER TWENTY-FIVE

HEL

Far down beneath the root of Yggdrasil, in darkest and coldest

Niflheim, lies the fearful domain of Hel,daughter of Loki and Angerboda. One half of her body has a livid tinge, and the other half the hue of human flesh; she is harsh and cruel, greedy for prey, and tenacious of those who have once fallen under her rule. The dark, deep vales surrounding her kingdom are called Hell-Ways; to go thither men must cross the river Gjoll ("roaring," "resounding"), spanned by the Bridge of Gjoll, which is paved with gold. Lofty walls enclose her dwelling place, and the gate that opens upon it is called Hell-Gate. Her hall is known as Eljudnir; her dish or porringer, as Hunger; her knife, as Famine; her bondman and bondmaid, as Ganglati and Ganglt (both words meaning "tardy"); her threshold, as Sinking to Destruction; her couch, as Sickbed; the curtains of her bed, as Glimmering Mischance. Her huge bandog, Garm, is bloody of chest and muzzle. Her "sooty-red" cock crows to herald the fall of the universe. In the midst of Niflheim stands the well Vergelmir,[1] beside which lies the serpent Niddhogg. The brinks of Vergelmir are called Nastrand (the Strand of Corpses); here is the most forbidding spot in Niflheim. All who did not fall in battle were said to go to Hell; but the general belief seems nevertheless to have been that only the wicked found their way thither.

In the terminology of the skalds, Hel is not infrequently designated as the Daughter of Loki, the Wolf's (the Fenris Wolf's) Sister, and the like. The names Hell (and Niflhel) are often used of the realm of the dead; thence the expression in Norwegian, *å slåihjel* (*ihel*), — "to strike into Hell," "to kill." When ghosts walked abroad, the saying might commonly be heard, "Hell-Gate is open" (*hnigin er helgrind*); for then it was possible for spirits to slip out.

CHAPTER TWENTY-SIX

THE GIANTS

The Giants, sworn enemies of men and of Æsir, were savage and violent but not always malicious. On occasion they might even manifest downright simplicity and good nature. They were of monstrous size, they often had several heads and hands, and they had dark skin and hair. Many of their women were well-favored, as for example Gerd; others again were most hideous: one might have a tail, another two heads, and so forth. The Giants owned great herds of cattle, bulls with gold horns, sheep, horses, and dogs. They loved darkness and the deeds of darkness; their women, avoiding the light of day, were in the habit of riding forth by night, and so they were sometimes called Dark-Riders or Night-Riders. If the sun's rays chanced to strike a Giant, he turned at once to stone. Now and then it happened that the Giants fought among themselves, throwing huge boulders at one another; but for the most part they were occupied in battle against mankind and the Æsir. The sanctuaries dedicated to the gods were most obnoxious to them, and when the Æsir gave ground before God and his saints, the hatred of the Giants spent itself on the newer deities. Long after the introduction of Christianity, the Giants survived in popular beliefs, and a multitude of legends bear witness to the hostility of the Giants against churches and church bells. To this day in many localities legends are current connected with great boulders or even mountains which are said to have been hurled at churches by the Giants. In earlier times they had as opponents Thor and Odin; later they did battle with mighty saints, with the archangel Michael, and above all with Saint Olaf. To the present day, tradition has preserved legends about fat and well-fed cattle — always black — owned by Mountain-Trolls or Jutuls, about Giant women with long tails which they find it impossible to conceal, and about the malice and stratagems of these beings toward mankind, whom they frequently entice to themselves into the mountains.

The Giants were skilful builders, wise and experienced in all the occult arts. When they became angry, a so-called Giant valor seized them which made their strength double what it was before. As already explained, the Giants lived in Jotunheim or in mountains lying nearer the haunts of men. More than ordinary fame attaches to Utgard, the Giant counterpart to the Midgard of mankind. The river Iving, which never froze over, marked the boundaries between Giants and gods. When the expeditions into the Arctic seas of the North began, Jotunheim or Giant-land gave its name to a real country: the great Russian steppes about the White Sea or Gandvik (the Bay of Trolls), or more particularly the regions bordering on the river Dwina. Here ruled the Giant kings, Geirrœd and his brother Godmund of Glæsisvoll; and many a daring voyager who visited them had surpassing dangers to encounter. The actual ruler of Utgard, however, was the crafty Utgard-Loki.

CHAPTER TWENTY-SEVEN

THE DWARFS

The Dwarfs and the Dark-Elves, between whom a sharp distinction was not always drawn, lived far beneath the surface of the earth or else made their habitat within great rocks or mounds. They were small of stature and ill-favored; the Dark-Elves were commonly reputed to be blacker than pitch. A large number of Dwarfs are mentioned by name in ancient literature; an interpolated passage in the *Voluspá* lists a long array of them, among others their chief Modsognir (or Motsognir?), and next in order after him, Durin. Other Dwarfs were Brokk,[1] Dvalin, and the four whom Odin appointed to hold up the vault of the heavens, namely North, East, South, and West. The chief occupation of the Dwarfs was that of smith, in which they had no rivals. All the most notable weapons and all the precious gems mentioned in the oldest myths were the work of cunning Dwarfs. The Dwarfs hated both gods and men and were unwilling to do them service; if nevertheless they were compelled to do so, they strove to give their handiwork some magic quality of evil omen so that it brought little joy to any one who came into possession of it.

CHAPTER TWENTY-EIGHT

THE VETTIR

All supernatural beings, good and evil alike, had one name in common, Vettir (*vœttir*, *véttir*, "spirits," "sprites"), which is still to a certain extent in use. The good ones were called Kind Sprites (*hollar vœttir*), and the evil ones were called Bad Sprites (*meinvœttir*, *úvœttir*). To the Kind Sprites belonged the so-called Land-Sprites, guardian divinities of a given country. In Iceland the Land-Sprites were held in high esteem; according to the earliest legal code ("Ulfljot's Law"), it was forbidden to sail a ship of war into any Icelandic harbor bearing at the prow a "gaping head or snout," which might terrify the Land-Sprites. The worst misfortune one could bring to a man was to invoke upon him the hostility of the Land-Sprites. This was exactly what Egil Skallagrimsson did when to gain revenge he raised a "libel-pole" against Erik Bloody-Axe. Before sailing away from Norway, Egil went ashore on an island lying far out to sea. As the story runs: "Egil walked up on the island. Carrying a hazel pole in his hand, he made his way to a rocky headland looking out upon the mainland. Taking a horse's head, he fixed it on top of the pole. Then, making use of a certain formula (a curse), he spoke thus, 'Here I erect this libel-pole, and I turn the libel against king Erik and queen Gunnhild,' — and with these words he turned the horse's head toward the mainland —; 'I aim this libel against the LandSprites of this country, to the end that they shall go astray and that no one of them shall reach or find his dwelling until they have driven Erik and Gunnhild forth from the land.' Thereupon he drove the pole into a crevice and left it there. He also turned the head landwards, and on the pole he wrote runes containing all the words of this curse. Then he went on board his ship."

Among the Kind Sprites may be reckoned all Æsir, Vanir, and BrightElves; among the Bad Sprites, Giants, Dwarfs, and Dark-Elves. After the coming of Christianity, however, no distinction was made between the Sprites; either they were all regarded as evil, or at any rate they were supposed beyond doubt to imperil the salvation of any man who should remain their friend. The Catholic clergy made it a point to arouse hatred against all the race of Sprites rather than to break down men's reliance on them. Numerous myths eventually sprang up having to do with Sprites that had suffered expulsion by means of the chants, the prayers, or the holy water of the priests, and so perforce had abandoned their dwelling places in stones or mounds. Each spring during Ascension Week in the North, as everywhere else throughout Catholic Christendom, the priests walked in procession around meadows and fields, holy water and crucifix in hand, intoning prayers and benedictions, and thus compelling the Sprites to flee the cultivated acres. During this particular week[1] there were several processional days;[2] besides these, there were two fixed processional days: the "greater," on April 25th; and the "less," on May 1st. Ceremonies of just this sort lent themselves directly to the maintenance of belief in the Sprites; even in our own times traditions persist relating to "Sprite mounds" and "Sprite trees," sacred trees that no hand must touch, — where the Sprites not long since were accustomed to receive offerings of food.

Among more recent superstitions concerned with the lesser supernatural beings, those relating to Elves and Giants (Jutuls, Trolls, Mountain-Trolls) are by far the most prevalent. Among the Elves must be counted the Huldre Folk,[1] who occupy a conspicuous place in the superstitions of Iceland. These Elves have quite the appearance of human beings. They make their homes under ground or in the mountains, and are not always hostile toward men but at times rather amiable and friendly; for this reason they are occasionally given the designation Darlings.[2] Among the Norwegians, too, there are numerous stories about the Hidden Folk or the underground people (mound folk, mountain folk), and above all about the Huldre herself, the Hill-Lady. She is often malicious; but at other times she shows a friendly demeanor toward men, as when she appears before the herdsman and speaks and dances with him. The Hill-Lady is often very beautiful as seen from the front, an impression enhanced by her blue smock and white linen hood. From behind she is hideous: her back is hollowed out like a trough and she has a tail that she is never able to conceal.

She owns a large herd of fat cattle and dogs to shepherd them ("huldre dogs"). She sings and plays well, but always in a melancholy strain; her tunes are called the "Hill-Lady's harping."

The underground folk are unable to beget children with each other. For this reason they desire to decoy young men or women in order to wed with them. They also have a bad habit of stealing human children; instead they lay one of their own brats in the cradle, the so-called changelings.[1]

Other Sprites are the Nix and the Water-Sprite. They live in rivers and lakes, and in certain localities are considered evil beings; in Telemark, for example, traditional report has it that the Nix demands each year a human sacrifice and that he is impelled to draw down to himself persons who approach the water after nightfall. As a rule, however, these Water-Sprites are guileless and friendly; they are adept at playing the fiddle, and it is possible to induce them to teach the art. Having no hope of eternal salvation, they are melancholy of mood; but they are made happy when any one promises to bring about their redemption, and they often demand the prospect of heavenly bliss as a reward for instruction in playing the fiddle. When the Nix is heard moaning and groaning, it is an omen that some one is about to be drowned. The Nix is able to reveal himself under various guises: as a handsome young man with long hair, as a dwarf, or as an old graybeard.

Out in the ocean dwell Merman and Mermaid.

They too sing and play beautifully and entice human beings to their haunts. They have the power to foretell future events. The upper part of their bodies has a human shape and the lower part has the likeness of a fish; the Mermaid appears beautiful as long as she does not let her finny tail be seen.

Among the Sprites the Brownie (Modern Norwegian *Nisse*) occupies a position of his own. He is a small boy or a small man dressed in gray clothes and a red cap; the crown of his head remains always moist, and his hands lack thumbs. Lingering about the farmsteads, he makes himself most useful so long as he is well treated; but if he takes umbrage at his hosts, he is capable of causing a great deal of trouble. If the Brownie is pleased with his surroundings, he will help the stableboy feed the horses, will assist the milkmaid in the care of the cows, and will even steal from the neighbors both hay and food to supply the farm on which he lives; but if he grows dissatisfied, he will bewitch the cattle, spoil the food, and bring misfortunes of other kinds upon the house. It may happen that two Brownies from two different farms encounter each other in foraging for hay, and then they will perhaps start a spirited fight armed with wisps of the hay. On Christmas Eve prudent folk are accustomed to set out for the Brownie a dish of Christmas pudding.

Whenever a person in sleep felt a weight upon his chest or when he dreamed disquieting dreams, he had no doubt that the Nightmare or Incubus was abroad, that he was being "ridden" by the Nightmare.

According to one account the Nightmare has no head, and is in fact hardly anything more than a mere brown smock; according to another description she is an actual woman who has the faculty of moving about by night and pressing her weight upon the sleeper. Thus the Nightmare does not differ widely from the so-called Werewolves,[1] who by day are actual human beings, but who during the night assume the shape of wolves; in this guise they course about bent on sinister mischief, attacking people in sleep, exhuming and devouring corpses in the churchyards. An ancient legend connected with one of the first Yngling kings in Sweden, Vanlandi by name, relates that a witch named Huld came over him in the form of a Nightmare and choked him to death. So firmly rooted was the belief of our forefathers in such things that the old ecclesiastical law of Eidsifa contained the following provision: "If evidence shows that a woman rides (as a Nightmare) any man or his servants, she shall pay a fine of three marks; if she cannot pay, she shall be outlawed." Nightmare and Werewolf are obviously related to the Dark-Riders or Night-Riders already mentioned,[2] and during later times no great distinction was drawn between them. One who had the ability to disguise his outward semblance was, in the ancient phrase, "multiform" (*eigi einhamr*), and was sometimes also called "shapeshifter" (*hamhleypa*).

CHAPTER TWENTY-NINE

THE HEROES AND LIFE IN VALHALLA

Concerning the mighty deeds and the destinies of the gods much has here been recounted; much less concerning their daily life in Asgard with those of mankind who came into their fellowship. Both Freyja and Odin made the Heroes welcome: Freyja in Folkvang, and Odin in Vingolf and Valhalla. We learn nothing, however, as to which of these domains was to be preferred; we have evidence only as to the manner in which Odin and the Heroes fleeted the time in Valhalla. It would seem that men generally thought of Valhalla as the resort of the fallen Heroes; there they passed their days in mirth and gladness. Odin himself chose them through the Valkyries; and the foremost among them were welcomed by certain Æsir or by doughty elder Heroes who went forth to meet them. In Valhalla the Heroes amuse themselves day by day with battles and banquets. In the morning, donning their armor they sally upon the field to fight and kill one another; yet they rise again unharmed, sit down to eat and drink, and remain the best of comrades.

The Heroes are a great company, constantly increasing; but their number is never so great that they do not have enough to eat from the flesh of the boar Sæhrimnir. The cook, named Andhrimnir, each day boils the boar in a kettle called Eldhrimnir; but at evening the beast is lust as much alive and unhurt as before. The Heroes drink ale and mead poured out for them by the Valkyries; Odin alone and those whom he desires to honor drink wine. All the mead they drink runs from the udder of Heidrun, a goat that stands on the roof of Valhalla cropping the branches of a tree called Lærad. The mead fills a great drinking-crock in the hall, enough of it to make all the Heroes drunken. Lærad possesses not only the inherent virtue of producing all the mead; on the roof of Valhalla there stands also a hart named Eikthyrnir, who gnaws at the tree and from whose antlers drops fall down into Vergelmir; thence flow forth twelve rivers that water the domain of the Æsir, and in addition thirteen other rivers.

CHAPTER THIRTY

CORRUPTION

In the morning of time, when Asgard and Valhalla were newly built, the gods lived in innocence, happiness and peace. "Glad in their courtyard they played at chess, nor of gold lacked aught"; so runs the description in the *Voluspá* of this golden age of the Æsir. Then came three mighty Thursar maidens out of Jotunheim, and enmity arose between Æsir and Vanir. One link in the chain of strife was the burning in Valhalla of a woman named Gullveig; "three times they burned the thrice born, again and againyet still she lives." The Æsir take counsel together to learn whether peace may still be preserved. Nothing can be done. Odin hurls his spear over the ranks of the enemy, and the first battle of the hosts begins. The walls of the Æsir stronghold are penetrated and the Vanir pour through the breach into Asgard. Yet eventually peace is declared between Æsir and Vanir, the story of which has already been told above.[1] Now the golden age of innocence is at an end; the gods are compelled to defend themselves against their foes, sometimes by the use of guile, as on the occasion when they tricked the Giant mason.[2] Other Giant women — Skadi and Gerd, for example — gain entrance to the dwellings of the Æsir, and Asgard's sanctity is no more. The season of tranquility gives way to a season of turbulent warfare, in which the gods more than ever before have need of magical weapons, of the aid of Heroes. The gods no longer rule the world as princes of peace; the most eminent of them become gods of war. To this period are to be referred the numerous myths having to do with valorous deeds and guileful practices; and the gods fall far short of always winning victory and glory. Corruption extends from gods to men; the divinities of battle, the Valkyries, ride forth into the world of mortals and here too peace is as a tale that is told.

CHAPTER THIRTY-ONE

THE TREASURES OF THE GOD

Loki's malice was in reality the occasion of the acquiring by the Æsir of all the precious weapons and treasures that served them in such good stead during their warfare with the Giants. Once upon a time Loki cut off all of Sif's hair. When Thor found out what had happened, he seized upon Loki and threatened to crush every bone in his body; he relented only on Loki's swearing that he would get the Dark-Elves to fashion for Sif hair from gold that would grow like other hair. Loki went with his task to certain Dwarfs known as the Sons of Ivaldi; and they, made not only the hair but also the ship Skidbladnir and the spear Gungnir. Loki promptly laid a wager of his own head with another Dwarf, named Brokk, that the Dwarf's brother Sindri was not craftsman enough to make three other talismans as precious as these. Brokk and Sindri repaired to the smithy, where Sindri, laying a pig's hide in the forge, asked Brokk to blow the bellows without pause until he himself returned to take the hide out again. No sooner had Sindri gone than a fly alighted on Brokk's arm and stung him; he kept the bellows going nevertheless, and when Sindri lifted his workmanship from the forge, it turned out to be a boar with golden bristles. Next he laid some gold in the forge, asked Brokk to blow as before, and went away; at once the fly came back, settled on Brokk's neck, and stung him twice as hard as the first time. Brokk notwithstanding held out until Sindri returned and lifted from the forge the gold ring Draupnir. Then he laid some iron in the fire and asked Brokk to blow, insisting that the work would be spoiled if the blowing stopped; but the fly came once more, settled between Brokk's eyes, and stung him on the eyelids so that the blood ran down and blinded him. He could not refrain from loosing his hold on the bellows with one hand to drive the fly away. Just at that moment the smith returned and declared that his handiwork had been on the very point of coming to naught; he lifted it from the forge, and it proved to be a hammer. Giving all three pieces to Brokk, he told him to make his way to Asgard and demand payment of the wager. The Æsir took their places on the judgment seats and came to the decision that Odin, Thor, and Frey were to judge between Loki and Brokk. Loki gave to Odin the spear Gungnir, which never failed of its mark; to Thor he gave the golden hair, which took root as soon as it was fixed on Sif's head; and to Frey he gave the ship Skidbladnir, which always found favoring winds and which could be folded up and placed in a pocket as occasion might befall. Brokk gave to Odin the ring Draupnir, from which each ninth night there dropped eight other rings as heavy as itself. To Frey he gave the boar Gullinbusti, who was able to run through the air and over the sea more swiftly than any horse; no night was so black, no murky region so dark as not to be illumined by his passage, so powerful was the light that shone from his bristles. To Thor he gave the hammer Mjollnir; with it he could strike as hard a blow as he pleased at anything that came in his way, and yet the hammer suffered not the least dent; he could throw it so as always to hit what he aimed at, and the hammer would return to his hand of its own power; when he so desired, he could make it small and put it in his pocket; he had but one fault to find: the shaft was rather short. The Æsir promptly judged that Brokk had won the wager; in Mjollnir they had acquired the very best defence against the Rime-Thursar. Loki wanted to redeem his head, but the Dwarf would not consent. "Catch me if you can," said Loki; and no sooner had he spoken than he was far away, for he wore shoes that could carry him through the air and over the seas. The Dwarf asked Thor to seize him, and Thor did so. Brokk was about to cut off Loki's head, but Loki declared that the wager called for his head only, and not for his neck. Brokk then began sewing Loki's lips together. He was unable to make an incision with his own knife, but with his brother's awl he managed to make openings through which, he could sew the mouth up tight; that done, he tore out through the lips the thong he had used in sewing them together.

THE RAPE OF IDUN

The story has already been told[2] of how the Giantess Skadi was received into the society of the Æsir and of how Njord was given to her as a husband by way of recompense for the murder of her father Thjazi. Loki's wiles provided the direct occasion for these events. Once upon a time Odin, accompanied by Loki and Hœnir, set forth on a journey that took them across mountains and over wastes where it was no easy matter to find food. At length, on descending into a valley, they caught sight of a drove of oxen; seizing one of the herd they kindled a fire, and began to boil the flesh. When they supposed the meat to be cooked, they took it off the fire; but it was far from done, and they had to let it boil a while longer. The same thing happened a second time; so they fell to debating the strange occurrence and wondering what might be the cause. As chance would have it, they were sitting under a tree, and so they heard a voice above their heads saying that he who sat perched in the tree was to blame for the tardiness of their cooking. Looking more closely, they saw an immense eagle. The eagle said that if they would allow it to still its hunger from the flesh of the ox, the meat would be cooked soon enough. They gave their consent, and the eagle forthwith swooped down and made off with both of the two hind quarters and both fore quarters. Loki became so angry that he picked up a staff and struck at the eagle. The eagle flew away, and one end of the staff stuck fast to the body of the bird and the other end remained fixed to Loki's arms, so that he was dragged over stock and stone till he thought his arms would be pulled from their sockets. He begged the eagle for mercy, but was not freed until he had given his promise to steal Idun out of Asgard, and her apples to boot. Not before he had sealed his promise with an oath was he permitted to return to his companions. When they had come back to Asgard and the appointed hour was at hand, he told Idun that he had discovered certain apples in a wood lying beyond the bounds of Asgard; she would no doubt find them worth having, and accordingly she would do well to visit the spot, taking her own apples along as a means of comparison. Idun permitted herself to be hoodwinked, and the eagle promptly came and carried her off. The eagle, none other than the Giant Thjazi in disguise, bore her away to his own estate of Thrymheim, where he kept her a long while in durance. The Æsir soon noticed that Idun's apples were gone, for they grew old and gray and could find no means of renewing their youth. They met in solemn conclave to inquire into the disappearance of Idun; then some one told that he had seen her walk forth from Asgard attended by Loki. The gods summoned Loki before the assembly and threatened him with death or dire tortures. He became so frightened that he promised to bring Idun back again if Freyja would only lend him her falcon disguise. His request being granted, he flew off to Jotunheim and arrived at Thrymheim at a time when Thjazi happened to be out at sea engaged in fishing, and Idun was alone at home. Loki transformed Idun into a nut and made off with her as fast as he could fly; but just afterward Thjazi returned, and not finding Idun, assumed the shape of an eagle and set out in pursuit of Loki. Little by little the eagle gained on the falcon. When the Æsir saw the two birds drawing near in their flight, they made haste to gather a heap of shavings outside the walls of Asgard, and at the very moment the falcon came inside they kindled the fire. The eagle was unable to come to a stop before it was directly above the bonfire; its wings bursting into flame, it was incapable of continuing the flight. Thus the Æsir got Thjazi into their power and put him to death just within the gates of Asgard.

Thjazi was one of the most formidable of the Giants. His father Olvaldi's wealth was so great that when Thjazi and his two brothers, Idi and Gang, were to divide their patrimony, they were compelled to measure out the gold by mouthfuls. When Thjazi's daughter Skadi came to demand payment of a penalty for the death of her father, she was not satisfied with being permitted to choose a husband[1]; she required in addition that the Æsir should make her laugh, something she deemed to be impossible. Loki again was called upon to deal with the emergency; so he played some vulgar tricks with a goat, and she was compelled to laugh in spite of herself. Odin took Thjazi's two eyes and tossed them up into the heavens, where they became two stars.

CHAPTER THIRTY-THREE

THOR'S UNLUCKY JOURNEY TO JOTUNHEIM

Thor, god of thunder, was the most ardent enemy of the Giants; yet he did not always come out the victor in his encounters with them. Once upon a time he drove off with his goats, attended by Loki; as night fell, they found lodging with a countryman. Here Thor slaughtered his goats, flayed them, and caused them to be cooked; then he invited the countryman, with his wife, his son, and his daughter, to share the meat with him, but asked them to throw all the bones down on the goats' hides. They did as he bade them, all but Thjalfi, the farmer's son, who broke a thigh bone to get at the marrow. At dawn Thor rose, donned his garments, raised Mjollnir aloft, and with the hammer consecrated the goats' hides; at once the goats sprang to their feet, as much alive as ever, except that one of them halted on one hind leg. Then Thor understood that the countryman or some one in his house had been careless enough to break the thigh bone; in anger he knitted his eyebrows and gripped the hammer so tightly that his knuckles grew white. The countryman, and his whole family with him, begged for mercy and offered in recompense all that they possessed. When Thor saw how frightened they were, his wrath cooled and he allowed himself to be appeased. By way of ransom he agreed to take the countryman's two children, the son Thjalfi and the daughter Roskva; and these two have followed him ever since.

Leaving his goats with the countryman, Thor continued on his journey to Jotunheim. He reached the seashore, crossed the deeps of the ocean, and stepped on land once more with his followers. Soon they came to a great forest, which they traversed all day until darkness fell. Thjalfi, swift of foot, carried Thor's wallet filled with food, for there was little to be picked up on the way. When night came, they looked about for a lodging and discovered an immense cabin, with a door on one side just as wide as the cabin itself. They went inside and lay down to sleep. At midnight they felt an earthquake so violent that the whole building shook; Thor roused his companions and bade them go into a smaller room through a door in the middle of the wall; as for himself, he sat down at the threshold with Mjollnir in his hand. A dreadful din and rumbling filled his ears. In the morning he went out and saw a gigantic man lying snoring near by in the wood; then he understood what had caused all the noise he had heard. He buckled on his belt of strength but just at that moment the man awoke, and for once, so it is said, Thor found himself little disposed to strike a blow. Instead, he asked the man his name. The man answered: "My name is Skrymir, and small need have I to ask for your name; I know you are Asa-Thor. But what have you done with my glove?" With these words Skrymir bent down to pick up his glove, and Thor saw that what he had taken by night to be a cabin was nothing else than Skrymir's glove, and that the penthouse was the thumb. "Shall we not travel together?" asked Skrymir. "Yes," said Thor. Before starting they ate their breakfasts, each party by itself, Skrymir from his own wallet, Thor and his companions from theirs; then Skrymir proposed that they put their food together in one sack. Thor gave his consent, and so Skrymir tied both their victuals and his own in a bag, which he slung on his back. He walked before them with tremendous paces during the day and at evening chose a night's lodging for them beneath a huge oak tree. "Here I am going to lie down to sleep," he said; "you may take the wallet and eat your supper." Skrymir fell asleep at once and was soon snoring heavily. Thor set about untying the wallet, but with very little success; when he had struggled a long while with his task, he grew angry, seized Mjollnir in both hands, and struck Skrymir on the head. Skrymir awoke and asked if a leaf had not fallen on his head. "Have you had your supper?" he asked. "Yes," replied Thor; "we are just going to bed." In the middle of the night Thor again heard Skrymir snoring so that the whole forest rang with the sound; he stepped up to him, lifted the hammer high in the air, and struck the man such a blow on the crown that the beak of the hammer sank far into the skull. Skrymir woke and asked: "What is up now? Was that an acorn that dropped on my head? How are you faring, Thor?" Thor hurried away, saying that he had just waked up and that the hour was hardly past midnight. "If I might only strike him a third time," thought Thor to himself, "he should never see the light of day again."

He kept watch until Skrymir once more fell asleep a little before morning, then ran up to him, and with all his might struck him in the temple so that the hammer sank into his skull up to the very handle. Skrymir sat up, stroked his cheek with his hand, and said: "There must be birds sitting in the tree above me; something dropped from the branches upon my head. Are you awake, Thor? It is time to get up now, and you have only a little distance to go to reach the stronghold of Utgard. I have heard you whispering among yourselves that I am not exactly small of stature, but you will see bigger men when you arrive at Utgard. And by the way, let me give you a piece of good advice: Do not be too arrogant; Utgard-Loki's men do not put up with much bragging from small boys. Else you had better turn back again, and that might be the wiser thing to do after all. But if you must and will go farther, walk toward the east; my way lies north, toward the mountains you see yonder." With these words Skrymir picked up the bag of food, slung it on his back, and strode off into the forest; and the Æsir were very glad to be rid of him.

Thor and his followers walked on until midday. Then they caught sight of a castle standing in the plain; but they had to bend their necks till their heads touched their backs before they were able to look over the top of it. The portals were barred with a gate that they could not unlock; but they crept in between the wickets and, seeing a huge hall, bent their steps toward it. The door stood open. They walked inside and there saw many men, all of immense size, sitting on benches. Among them sat the king, Utgard-Loki. They saluted him, but he only laughed scornfully, and asked if the little boy was not Riding-Thor. "You are no doubt bigger than you seem to be," he said; "but what kind of manly exercises do you and your traveling companions know? No one is allowed to sojourn here with us who is not able to do something or other better than any one else." Loki, who was standing behind the rest, spoke up: "There is one sport in which I am ready to try conclusions at once; nobody here is able to eat faster than I." UtgardLoki answered, "We shall soon find out." Then he commanded a man named Logi to step forward from the end of the bench to the middle of the floor to match his skill in eating against Loki's. A trencher full of meat was carried in and placed on the floor; Loki and Logi sat down, one at each end of the trencher, and ate with all their might. They met in the middle of the trencher; but while Loki had eaten only the meat, Logi had consumed the meat, the bones, and the trencher to boot. So Loki was beaten at this game. "What is that young fellow there able to do?" asked Utgard-Loki. "I will try running a race with some one," answered Thjalfi. "You will need to be swift of foot," said Utgard-Loki; then he went out into the field and asked a little fellow named Hugi to run against Thjalfi. In the first race Hugi was so far ahead that he turned back at the goal to meet Thjalfi. "You had better stretch your legs a bit more if you want to win," said Utgard-Loki; "for that matter, no swifter runner than you has ever visited us." In the second race Hugi reached the goal and turned while Thjalfi still had a long bowshot to run. "A very pretty heat," said Utgard-Loki; "yet I can hardly believe that Thjalfi would win if you two ran a third time." They ran once more; but when Hugi had reached the goal and turned around, Thjalfi had not covered half the course. All agreed that this contest might very well be regarded as finished. "What kind of manly sport are you going to favor us with, Thor?" asked Utgard-Loki; "we have heard great things about your prowess." "I will drink with any one that cares to drink," answered Thor. "Very good," said Utgard-Loki; then he went into the hall and asked his cupbearer to take down the great horn that the king's men were sentenced to drink from when they had done amiss. "We consider it well done," said Utgard-Loki, "if a man is able to empty this horn at one draught; some require two; but no one is such a weakling that he cannot drain it in three draughts." Looking at the horn, Thor did not think it very large but rather long; thirsty as he was, he placed it to his lips, drank deep, and thought to himself that he should probably not have to bend his head to the horn again. But when he stopped and looked to see how much he had drunk, it seemed to him that there was left not much less than there was before. "You have drunk pretty well," said Utgard-Loki, "but no great amount; to be sure, if any one had told me that Asa-Thor was no better drinker, I should not have believed it; but I am sure you will empty the horn at the second draught." Thor answered not a word, but took as long a pull as he possibly could; still the other end of the horn had not risen as high as he might have wished. When he paused it seemed to him that the level had sunk even less than before, yet now it was possible at least to carry the horn without spilling any of the liquor. "If you care to drink a third time, you have left the greater part till the last," said Utgard-Loki; "but if you are not more skilled in other games than in this, you cannot hope to earn as great a name among us as you have among the Æsir." Thor grew angry and placed the horn to his lips once more. He drank with all his might and kept drinking as long as ever he was able; when he paused to look, he could see that the level had sunk a little, but he did not want to drink any more. "It is easy to see," said Utgard-Loki, "that you are not so great a man as we supposed. Perhaps you would like to try your luck at other exercises, since you have had such bad luck with this one?" Thor answered, "I am willing to risk it; but unless I am much mistaken my drinking would have earned praise at home among the Æsir." Utgard-Loki replied "Our young boys sometimes find amusement in lifting my cat off the ground; it is only a small matter, and I should not have thought of proposing such a thing to Thor if I had not seen with my own eyes that you are far from being as mighty as I had supposed." A large gray cat ran out upon the floor of the hall. Thor stepped forward, took hold with one hand under her belly, and lifted; but the more he pulled, the more the cat bent herself into a bow; and when Thor had stretched his hand up as far as he could stretch, the cat raised only one foot off the floor. So Thor was worsted at this game too. Utgard-Loki declared that he might have known as much beforehand, since Thor was small of stature as compared with the big men around him. "Let one of them come out and wrestle with me if you think I am so small," answered Thor, "for now I am really in bad humor." "Not a man in the hall would demean himself so far as to take a turn with you," said Utgard-Loki, "but I will call in my old foster mother, Elli." She accordingly came in and grappled with Thor; but the more Thor tightened his hold, the firmer she stood; at last she began to use tricks of her own, and in the end Thor perforce sank down on one knee. "Perhaps that will do," said Utgard-Loki; "Thor will hardly challenge any one else here to a wrestling match." With these words he showed Thor and his companions to their seats. They remained there the rest of the night, and were entertained with the utmost hospitality. In the morning they rose and prepared to continue their journey. Utgard-Loki himself came in and caused a table to be spread for them, laden with all kinds of food and drink. Then they set forth on their way. Utgard-Loki accompanied them out of the castle and, as they were about to depart, asked Thor what he thought of the outcome of his expedition. Thor answered that he knew he had added nothing to his fame and that he felt the keenest disappointment to think that he was leaving behind him the reputation of a mere weakling. "Now I will tell you the truth," said Utgard-Loki, "since you are well outside of the castle. Never with my consent, so long as I live and rule, shall you be allowed to enter it again. And you would never have gained entrance if I had known how strong you were; for you came very near bringing the greatest misfortune upon us. The fact is, you have all been hoodwinked. It was I that you met in the forest; I tied the wallet with troll-iron so that you might not guess how to open it. Each single blow that you struck would have killed me outright if, unknown to you, I had not interposed for my protection the huge mountain you beheld outside the stronghold; there you may see even now three valleys, the one deeper than the other, all of them marks of your blows. The like happened with the games you played: Loki was hungry and ate very well, but Logi (*logi* = flame) was none other than fire itself turned loose, which consumed at one time both meat and trencher. Hugi, the fellow with whom Thjalfi ran his races, was my own thought (*hugr*), which of course was the fleeter of the two. When you drank from the horn, the wonder grew till I could not trust my own eyes; for the other end lay out in the ocean itself. If you look closely you can see how the level has sunk; that is what we call ebb tide. When you lifted the cat, we were all alarmed; she is the Midgard Serpent that encompasses all lands, but you raised her so high that head and tail barely touched the floor together. The wrestling match with Elli was no less a marvel, for never a man lived, nor ever shall live, but must fall before her (*elli* = old age). Now we are to part, and it were best for both of us that you never came back; for the future I will not fail to be on my guard against arts of that kind." Thor lifted his hammer, meaning to smite Utgard-Loki, but in a twinkling he had disappeared. Nor was Thor able again to catch sight of the castle; and so he had to return to Thrudvang. Yet before long he was bound on another expedition, this time against the Midgard Serpent itself.

THOR"S VISIT TO HYMIR

THOR'S VISIT TO GEIRRŒD

Once upon a time, as Loki was flying about for sport in Frigg's falcon disguise, he was taken with a desire to see how matters stood on the estates of Geirrœd. Settling on a window ledge, he looked into the hall. Geirrœd bade one of his men take the bird captive; but this was more easily said than done, and Loki was vastly amused at the proposal. He therefore remained sitting on his perch for a while, thinking there would be time enough to escape when the man had clambered up; but when Loki wanted to fly away, his feet clung to the wall and so he was taken in the toils. Geirrœd, on examining his eyes, knew that it was no real bird, but a shape-shifter; he spoke to Loki but received no answer. Geirrœd then locked him up in a chest, where he left him for three months without food. Finally he took him out again, and Loki was compelled to reveal who he was. To save his life he promised to induce Thor to pay a visit to the farmstead of Geirrœd without his hammer, his belt of strength, or his gauntlets. It is not known how Loki managed this affair, but certain it is that Thor set forth on the journey. Loki and Thjalfi went with him. On the way Thor sojourned for a time with the Giantess Grid, who was the mother of the god Vidar and as such a friend of the Æsir. From her Thor learned that Geirrœd was a crafty Giant, with whom it was no simple matter to deal. Accordingly she made Thor a loan of a belt of strength, a pair of iron gauntlets, and her own staff, the "Grid-Staff" (*Gríðarvolr*; *volr* = staff). Thor presently arrived at the banks of a great river called Vimur, across which he was compelled to wade. Girdling on his belt, he braced himself against the current by means of the staff, while Loki held fast to the belt. By the time he had reached midstream, the water flowed over his shoulders. Then quoth Thor:

Wax no more, Vimur;

My purpose holds to wade To the very home of the Giants.

Know this, that as thy waxing Will wax my Æsir power,
Even as high as the heavens.

Soon he became aware that Geirrœd's daughter Gjalp was standing astride the river where it narrowed between rocky walls, and that the swelling of the waters was her work. He picked up a boulder from the bed of the stream and threw it at her, saying, "A river must be dammed at the mouth." The boulder found its mark, and now the current bore him so close to the bank that he was able to catch hold of a mountain ash, by the aid of which he pulled himself ashore. From this incident comes the saying, "The mountain ash is the salvation of Thor." Thjalfi — according to a skaldic poem[1] — had seized the thong of Thor's shield and effected his passage in this way. When Thor arrived at Geirrœd's house, he and his companions were lodged in a goat-house[2] where there was but a single chair. Thor sat down in it, but soon noticed that it was being raised with him toward the roof. He thrust the Grid-Staff up against a beam and let all his weight sink heavily into the chair, whereupon there at once arose from below a great crashing and wailing; the din came from Gjalp and Greip, the two daughters of Geirrced, who had lain beneath the chair and whose backs he had thus broken. Then quoth Thor:

Once I made use
Of my Æsir might,
Yonder in the home of the Giants;
That was when Gjalp and Greip,
Daughters of Geirrœd,
Would fain lift me up to the heavens.

Now Geirrœd called Thor into the hall to make trial of his prowess in games of skill. Great fires were burning lengthwise of the room, and just as Thor passed in front of Geirrœd, the Giant picked up with his tongs a glowing bolt of iron and threw it at him. Thor caught it in his iron gauntlet and raised it aloft, but Geirrœd leaped for refuge behind a pillar. Thor hurled the bolt with such force that it went through the pillar, through Geirrœd and the wall, and then buried itself in the earth.

CHAPTER THIRTY-SIX

THOR'S COMBAT WITH RUNGNIR

Once upon a time, when Thor had gone off to the east to kill Trolls, Odin rode on Sleipnir's back into Jotunheim and pressed forward to the dwelling of the Giant Rungnir. Rungnir inquired who the gold-helmeted man might be, who was thus able to ride both air and sea — he must be the master of a good horse! Odin undertook to wager his head that the horse's like was not to be found in all Jotunheim. Rungnir retorted that his own horse, Goldmane, was the swifter of the two; with these words he sprang on his horse in a rage and rode in pursuit of Odin to pay him for his boasting. Odin struck spurs into Sleipnir and maintained his lead; but Rungnir had lashed himself into such a Giant fury that before he knew it he had passed within the gates of Asgard. The Æsir immediately invited him to sit down with them at their drinking, to which he assented and walked into the hall. The beakers were brought forward from which Thor was in the habit of drinking; Rungnir emptied them all without a murmur, and becoming drunk, began to vaunt himself. He would pick Valhalla up bodily and carry it off to Jotunheim; he would level Asgard with the earth and put all the gods to death but Freyja and Sif, and these two he would bear away to his own house. He insisted that Freyja alone had the courage to fill his beaker, and that he would make short work of drinking up all of the Æsir's ale. The Æsir, eventually growing weary of his bragging, summoned Thor; without a moment's delay Thor was on the spot, brandishing his hammer and fuming with anger. Thor demanded to know who had permitted foul Giants to drink there, who had allowed Rungnir to remain in Valhalla, and why Freyja was filling his cup as if it was a banquet for the gods. Rungnir turned unfriendly eyes on Thor and answered that Odin in person had invited him to enter and had given him safe conduct. Thor declared that before the Giant made his escape he would have reason to rue that invitation. "Thor would gain little glory by killing an unarmed man," said Rungnir; "but have you courage enough to fight with me at the boundary stones of Grjottunagard? I was a fool to forget my shield and whetstone at home, for if I had my weapons at hand we could fight it out at once; but if you kill me while I am unarmed, you will be every man's byword for cowardice." That was the first time any one had offered to stand against Thor in single combat, and so he immediately accepted the challenge. Rungnir rode off at top speed; when he arrived at home in Jotunheim, the Giants paid him the highest compliments on his courage. They realized, none the less, how much was at stake: if Rungnir, their most powerful champion, should be worsted, they might look for all manner of mischances. Accordingly they set about the task of making a man of clay, nine miles tall and three miles broad beneath the arms. They were unable to find a heart large enough for him until it occurred to them to make use of the heart of a mare. Rungnir for his part had a three-cornered heart of stone; his head also was of stone, and his shield as well. Taking his position behind his shield he awaited at Grjottunagard the corning of Thor; resting his whetstone on his shoulder, he presented a most formidable figure. The clay Giant, on the contrary, who bore the name Mokkurkalfi, was so terrified that "he made water as soon as he caught sight of Thor." Thor came on the field seconded by Thjalfi. As they advanced Thjalfi called out, "You have made a reckless choice of position, Giant; Thor is closing in on you from below through the earth." Rungnir then placed his shield beneath his feet and stood on it; no sooner had he done so than Thor, heralded by a burst of thunder and lightning, came upon the scene in all his Æsir might and from a great distance hurled his hammer at the Giant. Rungnir gripped his whetstone with both hands and threw it at Thor, but it struck the hammer in mid air and was shattered to pieces. One part fell to the, ground, and from these fragments have come all the mountains of whetstone; the other part, piercing Thor's head, brought him to earth. The hammer struck Rungnir on the crown and smashed his skull to bits; he fell across the body of Thor so that his foot rested on Thor's neck. By this time Thjalfi had won an easy victory over Mokkurkalfi. Neither Thjalfi nor any of the Æsir was able to lift Rungnir's foot off Thor's neck; but presently Magni came upon the field — the son of Thor and Jarnsaxa, a youngster of three years — and raised the Giant's foot as if in play; it was unfortunate, so he said, that he had not come sooner, in which case he would have struck the Giant dead with his bare fist. Thor rose to his feet and praised his son handsomely; he avowed that the boy in time would amount to something, and by way of reward made him a present of Rungnir's horse Goldmane. Odin, however, declared that Thor had not done right in giving so fine a horse to the son of a Giantess instead of to his own father.

Thor now returned to his home in Thrudvang, but the whetstone remained fixed in his head. To be rid of it he sought the aid of Groa, the wife of Aurvandil the Brave. The woman read magic spells over Thor's head until the whetstone loosened its hold. When Thor noticed what was happening, he wanted to please the woman in his turn; so he told her that, on a journey to the north, he had once waded across the Elivagar carrying Aurvandil in a pannier out from Jotunheim. In proof of his story he related that one of Aurvandil's toes, protruding out of the pannier, became so badly frostbitten that he was compelled to break it off; he then tossed it into the heavens, where it turned into a star that had since been called Aurvandil's Toe. No long time would pass, he added, before Aurvandil returned home again. Groa was so happy at hearing his tale that she forgot all about her magic spells; the whetstone consequently was not fully loosened, and so still protrudes from Thor's head. Therefore no whetstones must be thrown crosswise over the floor, for in that event the whetstone in Thor's head will be set in motion.

CHAPTER THIRTY-SEVEN

THRYM STEALS MJOLLNIR

At length it so happened that Thor found an opportunity to steal into Jotunheim and glut his hatred of the Giants. He had lain down to sleep, and when he awoke he missed his hammer. Enraged beyond bounds, he at once sought the advice of Loki, who promised to go out in search of the hammer provided Freyja would lend him her bird plumage. Freyja being willing, Loki flew off to Jotunheim and came into the presence of Thrym, king of the Thursar, who was sitting on a mound braiding gold cords for his dogs and clipping the manes of his horses. "What news among the Æsir? What news among the Elves? And what brings you to Jotunheim alone?" asked Thrym. "There is something wrong somewhere," Loki answered; "you do not happen to have hidden Thor's hammer, do you?" "Yes," retorted Thrym, "I have hidden it eight miles deep in the earth, and no man will get it before he brings me Freyja to wife." Loki brought the bad news back to Asgard. He then went with Thor to ask Freyja if she would consent to become the wife of Thrym; highly incensed, she gave them a curt "No" for answer. The Æsir accordingly met in conclave to determine what steps were to be taken; no one was able to suggest anything to the purpose until Heimdal proposed that they should dress Thor to take the place of Freyja, decking him out to that end with the Necklace of the Brisings and other appropriate ornaments. Thor pronounced the plan far beneath his dignity but at last gave in; so they dressed him in bridal linen, adorned him with the Necklace of the Brisings, hung jingling keys at his belt, put a kerchief on his head, and wrapped him in the long garments of a woman. Loki, in the habit of a handmaiden, followed in his train. Hitching Thor's goats to the cart, the two drove off at a pace that split mountains asunder and struck the earth into flames. As they drew near the domain of the Thursar king, Thrym bade the Giants rise to their feet and deck the benches for the coming of the bride. "In my possession are cows with gold horns, black bulls, heaps of treasure, and mounds of jewels," said Thrym; "Freyja is now my sole desire." When evening had come, food was borne in before the two guests. Thor by himself ate a whole ox, eight salmon, and all of the delicacies prepared for the women, and washed it all down with three crocks of mead. "Did any one ever see a bride take bigger and harder bites or drink more mead?" asked Thrym. "For eight days on end," answered Loki, "Freyja has not tasted a morsel, so great has been her longing after Jotunheim." Thrym now bowed his head beneath the kerchief to kiss the bride; but she shot such piercing glances upon him that he started back. "Why does Freyja look so grim? Her eyes dart fire." "Eight nights on end," answered Loki, "Freyja has not slept a wink, so great has been her longing after Jotunheim." Just at that moment the hideous old grandmother came in and asked for a bridal gift. Thrym gave commands that Mjollnir should be borne in and laid on the bride's lap so that the wedding might go forward. When Thor once more beheld his hammer, his heart laughed within him. First he slew Thrym, then the old beldame, and thereafter he crushed into atoms all the kindred of the Giants. Thus Thor got his hammer back again after all.

CHAPTER THIRTY-EIGHT

THE NECKLACE OF THE BRISINGS

On most of Thor's expeditions, Loki acted the part of a friend, outwardly at least. Between Heimdal and Loki, on the contrary, there was deadly enmity without ceasing. This enmity showed itself, for example, on the occasion when Loki had stolen the Necklace of the Brisings from Freyja. Loki hid the ornament in the sea at Singastein, and kept guard over it himself in the shape of a seal. Heimdal likewise assumed the likeness of a seal, and so compelled Loki to restore what he had stolen. This is the probable interpretation of the casual references in Snorri's *Edda*,[1] in which case we have here to do with the old and authentic form of the myth. A variant of the myth, quite different and far less primitive, is to be found in the legendary *Sorla þáttr*,[2] dating from the thirteenth century. According to this account, Freyja had received the necklace from four Dwarfs; Odin, however, coveting it, asked Loki to steal it for him. It would prove to be a difficult task, Loki said, for Freyja's house was so well built and so securely bolted that no one would be able to enter without her consent. Odin commanded him to make the attempt nevertheless, and Loki had to obey. When he arrived at the door he could not find even the smallest opening; taking the shape of a fly he crept about the lock a long time, until finally he discovered high up on the door a tiny crevice, through which he succeeded in making an entrance. Freyja lay asleep with the necklace about her neck, the lock facing downward; he accordingly transformed himself into a flea and bit her so hard on the cheek that she awoke and turned on the other side. The lock having in this way been made to face upward, he assumed his natural shape once more and made off with the ornament. Escaping through the door, which it was possible to open from the inside, he brought the treasure to Odin. Freyja, as soon as she awoke, noticed the theft and complained to Odin. He answered that she might have the necklace again on one condition: she was to stir up strife between two major kings so that they would wage unceasing war against each other, the fallen warriors constantly rising to fight again. This compact came to be the occasion of the Battle of the Hjadnings.

CHAPTER THIRTY-NINE

THE DEATH OF BALDUR

Amid confusion and struggle of various kinds life thus ran its course among the Æsir. Yet Balder still remained to them, the god of innocence and purity; while he survived, evil and violence could not gain supremacy in the universe. There came a time, however, when he began to be visited by disquieting dreams, which filled all the gods with foreboding. The Æsir and the goddesses held a general assembly to inquire into the meaning of these portents. Odin himself rode forth on Sleipnir into the very depths of Niflheim to take counsel with a departed sibyl or prophetess. He arrived at the high hall of Hell; and to the east of the door, where lay the grave of the sibyl, he took his station and chanted his incantations to waken the dead. The sibyl, compelled to rise from her grave, asked who had come to disturb her rest. "The snow covered me," she said, "the rain beat upon me, and the moist dews fell over me; I had long been dead." Odin answered, "I am named Vegtam, the son of Valtam; tell me now for whom Hel has adorned her hall." "For Balder the mead is brewed, and the Æsir are sore afflicted." "Who then shall bring death upon Balder?"

"Hod shall bring death to Balder," washer response. "Who shall avenge his death upon Hod?" asked Odin. "Rind shall bear a son (Vali) in the West-Halls," she replied; "he shall neither wash his hands nor comb his hair until he has brought Balder's slayer to the funeral pyre; one night old, he shall kill him." "Speak, be not yet silent," said Odin; "still more would I fain learn: who are the maidens that are weeping sorely and throwing their neckerchiefs into the air?" "Now I know that you are not Vegtam, as you have said, but Odin," answered the prophetess. "And you are neither sibyl nor wise woman; you are the mother of three Thursar." "Ride home again, Odin," said the prophetess, "and return to me when Loki has regained his freedom and the Twilight of the Gods is near at hand."

Frigg now bound all things by an oath that they would do Balder no harm-fire and water, iron and all manner of metals, rocks, earth, trees, maladies, beasts and birds, poisons and serpents. Now the Æsir, deeming themselves, secure, even found amusement at their assemblies in having Balder stand forward while the others shot missiles at him, aimed blows at him, or threw stones at him; whatever they might do, he suffered no wound. Loki, meanwhile, was not pleased. Assuming the shape of a woman, he paid a visit to Frigg at Fensalir. Frigg asked the woman what the Æsir were occupied with at their assembly. "They are all shooting at Balder without working him the least injury," she said. "Neither weapons nor trees will do him any harm, for I have bound all things by an oath." "Is it really true that all things have sworn to spare Balder?" the woman asked. "All things, except only a tiny sprig growing west of Valhalla, called Mistletoe (*mistilteinn*); I deemed it too young a thing to be bound by an oath." Now Loki went away, tore up the mistletoe, and carried it off to the assembly. Hod, because of his blindness, was standing at the outer edge of the circle. Loki asked him why he too was not shooting at Balder. "I cannot see where he is standing; and besides, I have no weapon," answered Hod. "Nevertheless, you ought to follow the example of the others," said Loki, "and thus pay equal honor to Balder. Take this wand and shoot at him; I will show you where he is standing." Hod grasped the mistletoe, took his position according to Loki's bidding, and let fly at Balder; the bolt sped directly through his body, and he sank down dead. Thus came about the greatest mischance that ever befell gods and men. When the Æsir saw Balder fall to the ground, they were speechless with fear, and none moved a finger to lift him up; they looked at one another, and all alike were filled with wrath at the man who had brought that deed to pass; yet they were powerless to avenge the murder, since the spot on which they stood had been solemnly set aside as a sanctuary. For a time they were unable to utter a word for weeping; Odin above all felt the full force of the blow, for he saw most clearly what a loss had befallen the Æsir through Balder's death. When the gods had in part regained their composure, Frigg asked who among the Æsir would undertake to gain her favor by riding the HellWays to seek speech with Balder and to learn from Hel what recompense she would demand for permitting Balder's release and his return to Asgard. Hermod the Bold, Odin's son, declared himself willing; having got the loan of Sleipnir for the journey, he mounted and took the road with the utmost speed.

The Æsir took Balder's body and bore it down to the sea. There lay his great ship, Ringhorni, drawn up on land; with the intention of using it for Balder's funeral pyre, they strove to launch it but were unable to move it from the spot. They were therefore compelled to send a messenger to Jotunheim to summon the Giantess Hyrrokkin, and she came riding to them mounted on a wolf, which she guided by vipers in lieu of reins. She dismounted, and Odin assigned four Berserks to the task of holding her steed; they could not restrain the wolf, however, before they had thrown it to the ground. The Giantess stepped to the prow of the boat, and at the first effort shoved it off so fast that the rollers burst into flame and the whole earth trembled. Thor, his wrath getting the better of him, wanted to crush her head, but all the other gods interceded on her behalf. Now the body of Balder was carried out onto the ship, and when his wife Nanna saw what was happening, her heart broke for sorrow; so her body also was laid on the pyre. The fire was then kindled and Thor came forward and consecrated the pyre with Mjollnir; just at that moment a Dwarf named Lit ran in front of him, and Thor spurned the Dwarf into the fire, where he too was burned. Beings of many kinds came to see the burning. First of all was Odin, and with him Frigg, the Valkyries, and Odin's ravens. Frey drove a cart drawn by the boar Gullinbusti, otherwise called Slidrugtanni. Heimdal rode his horse Goldtop, and Freyja drove her cats. Throngs of Rime-Thursar and Cliff-Ettins presented themselves likewise. Odin laid on the pile the ring Draupnir. Balder's horse also was led fully caparisoned onto the blazing ship.

In the meantime Hermod was on his way to Hell. Nine nights he rode through dark and deep valleys and saw nothing until he came to the river Gjoll and rode out onto the Bridge of Gjoll, which is paved with gleaming gold. A maiden named Modgud, who keeps watch over the bridge, asked his name and kindred. Then she told him that not many days before, five companies of dead men had ridden across the bridge; "and yet," she said, "it thunders as loudly beneath your paces alone as beneath the feet of all of them together. Nor have you the visage of a dead man; why are you riding alone on the way to Hell?" "I am riding to Hell," answered Hermod, "in search of Balder. Have you seen him pass along the Way of Hell?" She told him that Balder had already traversed the Bridge of Gjoll: "The Way of Hell lies downward and northward." Hermod rode on until he arrived at Hell-Gate. There he dismounted, tightened his saddle-girths, mounted once more, and struck spurs to his horse; the horse jumped so high above the gate that he did not so much as touch it with his hoof. Hermod rode straight to the hall, dismounted, and stepped inside; there he saw his brother Balder sitting in the high seat. He remained in the hall during the night; in the morning he asked Hel to permit Balder to ride away with him, telling her at the same time how great was the grief of the Æsir. Hel answered that she meant to assure herself beforehand whether Balder was really so much beloved as he was reputed to be. "If all things on earth," she said, "be they quick or dead, will weep for him, then he shall return to the Æsir; but if there is one thing that will not weep, he shall remain with me." Then Hermod arose, and Balder followed him out through the door and bade him give Odin the ring Draupnir in memory of him. Nanna gave into his charge a kerchief for Frigg and other gifts besides, and for Fulla a finger ring. Thereupon Hermod rode forth on his journey until he came back to Asgard, where he imparted to the gods all that he had seen and heard.

The Æsir now sent messengers throughout the whole world to ask all things to weep for Balder's release from Hell; all things did weep, men, beasts, earth, trees, and all manner of metals, and they can still be seen weeping whenever they pass from frost to heat. But when the messengers, their errand done, were returning home again, they discovered among the rocks a Giantess named Thokk; her too they asked to weep Balder out of the bounds of Hell but she replied:

Thokk shall weep Dry tears
On Balder's pyre.
Nor in life nor in death
Did Karl's son bring me joy; Hel hold what she hath!

Balder's homecoming thus came to naught. The Giantess was none other than Loki, who by such means finished his evil deed. Retribution, however, soon fell upon him. Upon Hod as well Balder's death was to be avenged; and according to the sibyl's decree to Odin, vengeance was to come at the hands of Vali, the son of Odin and Rind. The particulars of his doom are not recorded in the *Eddas*.

CHAPTER FORTY

ÆGIR'S BANQUET — THE CHASTISING OF LOKI

When Ægir had got possession of the huge kettle borrowed by Thor from Hymir, he prepared a great banquet for the Æsir.[1] Odin was one of the guests; others were Frigg, Sif, Bragi, Idun, Tyr, Njord, Skadi, Frey, Freyja, Vidar, Frey's serving men, Byggvir and Beyla, with a host of other Æsir and Elves besides. Loki also made one of the number, but Thor was absent on an expedition to the east. Radiant gold lit the room instead of tapers, and the ale poured forth of itself without the aid of any cupbearer. Ægir's servants, Eldir and Fimafeng, were praised highly on every hand for the skilful performance of their duty. Hereat Loki grew angry and killed Fimafeng, although the spot was holy ground. The Æsir brandished their shields, raised an outcry against Loki, and drove him out into the forest; then they sat down to their drinking. Loki nevertheless shortly returned and, meeting Eldir outside the hall, asked him what the Æsir were discoursing about over their cups. "They are speaking of their weapons and their valorous deeds," answered Eldir; "and none among them has a good word to say for you." Loki said that he purposed to go inside and look on at the banquet and that he intended to bring evil and dissension with him and to mingle misfortune with the mead they were drinking. Refusing to listen to Eldir's warnings, he forced his way with threats. All ceased speaking when they saw Loki enter. He asked permission to still his thirst and, no one answering a word, he demanded that they should either show him to a seat or drive him out once more. Bragi declared that the Æsir never would give him a place among them again; whereupon Loki reminded Odin that once in the morning of time they two had blended blood with each other and thus had become sworn brothers, on which occasion Odin had given his promise that no drink should cross his

lips that was not offered to both of them alike. Odin accordingly asked Vidar to make room for Loki at his side, and Vidar promptly arose and poured drink into Loki's cup. Loki offered obeisance to all the gods and goddesses and drank to them all — Bragi alone excepted. Bragi now proposed to present him with horse and sword and rings in recompense if he would keep the peace. Loki replied with taunts, maintaining that Bragi had none of the possessions of which he spoke: "Of all the Æsir sitting here, you are most afraid of battle and most wary of flying bolts." "If I were outside the hall, as certainly as I now sit within the hall, I should carry away your head in my hand," retorted Bragi. "You are brave enough while you are sitting in your seat, Bragi Grace-the-Benches," answered Loki; "if you are angry, come and fight it out with me." "I beg of you," said

Bragi's wife, Idun, "do not taunt Loki herein Ægir's hall." "Hold your tongue, Idun," rejoined Loki; "of all wanton women I call you the most wanton; with your white arms you have embraced the slayer of your own brother." Idun declared that she only wished to pacify Bragi so that the two would not come to blows. Now Gefjon spoke: "Why do you two Æsir continue to bandy words in this presence? Loki appears not to know that he is on the wrong road, that all the gods are angry at him." Loki at once stopped her lips by reminding her of an amorous adventure in which she had played a part. Hereupon Odin warned Loki to beware of Gefjon's wrath: "For she knows the destinies of men as well as I." Loki immediately turned upon Odin and said: "You have often granted victory to dastards." "You, for your part," replied Odin, "lived eight winters under ground as a woman, milking cows." No insult much worse could possibly be thrown in a man's teeth, and so Loki was not slow in making a rejoinder no less coarse, to the effect, namely, that Odin had once sojourned on the island of Samsey engaged in the practice of witchcraft and sorcery after the manner of witches. Frigg now took a part in the discussion, declaring that Odin and Loki had better not reveal what they had been occupied with in the morning of time, and Loki immediately countered with the old story that on a certain occasion when Odin was absent from home, she had had his brothers Vili and Ve for husbands. "Had I here in Ægir's hall a son like Balder, you would not easily escape," answered Frigg. "You plainly wish me to recount still more of my evil deeds," said Loki; "know then, it is my doing that you shall no more see Balder come riding into the hall." "You are beside yourself," said Freyja, "to dare relate all the evil and heinous acts of your life; Frigg knows the course of destiny, though she tells no man thereof." "Silence," answered Loki; "I know you only too well. There is scarcely any one in this company, whether of Æsir or Elves, whom you have not had for a lover; you are a Troll, wicked through and through; once the gods surprised you with your own brother." "It is of little consequence," said Njord, "that women have lovers; it is far worse that you, womanish god, venture into our presence." Loki reminded him that he had once been sent east ward as a hostage and that the women of Hymir had covered him with insults. "Even if I was once a hostage, nevertheless I have begotten a son (Frey) who is the friend of all and the bulwark of the Æsir." "His mother was your own sister," replied Loki. Tyr now spoke: "Frey is foremost of the brave men of Asgard, he violates neither maid nor wife, and he looses from bonds all those that are bound." "Hold your tongue, Tyr; never have you been able to bring about peace; do not forget how the Fenris Wolf tore off your right hand." "Nevertheless," answered Frey, "the Wolf lies in bondage until the Twilight of the Gods; and just as he lies chained outside the river's mouth, so may you come to lie fettered if you do not keep silence." "For gold you bought the daughter of Gymir and sold your sword besides, so that when the sons of Muspell come riding across the Dark Woods you will find no weapon ready to your hand." Then spoke Byggvir, Frey's serving man: "If I had offspring like that of Ingunar-Frey and if I lived happily as he does, I would crush this crow of evil omen finer than marrow and break all his limbs asunder." "What is that little thing wagging his tail and whimpering there under the mill? You hid yourself in the straw on the floor when men went forth to battle." On Heimdal's declaring Loki to be drunk, Loki replied: "Hold your tongue, Heimdal. In the morning of time a life most base was dealt out to be your portion, to stand forever with a stiff back, waking and watching on behalf of the gods." Skadi now forecast a threatening future for Loki: "Hitherto your lot has been good, Loki, but you shall not much longer play fast and loose; to the sharp stone the gods shall bind you with your own son's entrails." "None the less was I chief among those that put your father Thjazi to death," answered Loki. Skadi retorted, "Therefore cold counsels will always go out to you from my house and home." Now Sif stepped forward and poured mead into a horn for Loki; she drank to him and asked him to molest Skadi no more, but his only response was to boast that he, if none else, had enjoyed the favors of Sif. "The mountains are trembling," said Beyla; "I think Thor must be coming; he will find a way of stopping the mouth of him who heaps blame on the Æsir." As Loki was berating Beyla, Thor appeared and, fuming with rage, threatened Loki with his hammer. Still Loki had the boldness to say to him: "You will not be so brave when you go out against the Wolf, and the Wolf devours Odin." "I will hurl you into the regions of the east so that no man shall lay eyes on you again," answered Thor. "You had better keep quiet about your journeys to the east," said Loki, adding a further reminder of the cowardly way in which Thor had borne himself in Skrymir's glove and how fast he had found the thongs bound about the wallet; "hale and hearty, you nearly perished with hunger." "If you do not hold your tongue at once, Mjollnir shall strike you, without further ado, down to Hell, even lower than the Gate of Corpses." "I have spoken what I had to speak," said Loki; "I will now depart, on your account alone, for I know that you strike when you are moved to strike." To Ægir he declared that this banquet was his last, that flames were to consume all that he owned.

Loki now took his leave and hid himself in the mountains, where he built a house with four doors so placed that from within he was able to spy in all directions. Often he assumed the shape of a salmon and lurked among the waterfalls of Franang. He pondered much upon what devices the Æsir might employ in order to catch him in the falls; and as he sat in the house brooding on these things, he took flax yarn and wove it into meshes in the manner commonly used in making a net. Before long he saw the Æsir drawing near; for Odin, looking out from Lidskjalf, had discovered his hiding. Losing no time, Loki threw the net on the fire burning before him, and sprang into the waterfall. When the Æsir reached the house, the wise Kvasir was the first to enter; as soon as he saw the ashes of the burned net, he understood that it was a means of catching fish, and he told the Æsir as much. They all set about the task of making a net according to the model in the ashes; when it was finished they went down to the stream and threw the net into the water. Thor had hold of one end, and all the other Æsir held fast to the other end. As they drew the net, Loki swam before it and lay quiet between two stones until the net had passed over him; nevertheless they noticed that the net had touched some living thing. They went up stream and cast in the net a second time, but now they had weighted it so that nothing could pass beneath it. Loki swam ahead of the net until he came within a short distance of the sea; then he leaped over the rope and swam up to the waterfall again. Now the Æsir had caught sight of him; they went up stream a third time and separated into two parties so that each group held one end of the net while Thor waded down the middle of the river. In such a manner they drew the net down toward the sea. In this predicament Loki was compelled either to run out to sea, which would put him in grave danger of his life, or to leap over the, net once more. He ventured the leap anew, but Thor seized him and held him fast by the tail, although the salmon slipped a short way through his hands; this is the reason why the salmon tapers toward the tail. Now Loki was taken captive outside the bounds of any hallowed place, and therefore he could expect no mercy. The Æsir carried him off to a cavern in the mountains. There they took three flagstones, placed them on end, and bored a hole in each one. Next they seized hold of Loki's sons, Vali and Nari; Vali, transforming himself into a wolf, at once tore his brother limb from limb. Thereupon the Æsir took Nari's entrails and with them bound Loki in such a position across the three stones that one of the stones stood under his shoulders, the second under his loins, and the third under the tendons of his knees. The bands turned into iron. Skadi caught a venomous serpent and fixed it above him in such a way that the venom would be sure to drip into his face. Sigyn, Loki's wife, stood beside him holding a basin to catch the dripping poison; but when the basin was filled, she had to go away to empty it; and while she was gone the poison fell on his face and threw him into such violent contortions that the whole earth trembled. This is the phenomenon now known as an earthquake. Thus Loki shall lie bound until the coming of the Twilight of the Gods.

CHAPTER FORTY-ONE

OTHER NORSE MYTHS CONCERNING THE DEATH OF BALDER

The ancient Danish historian Saxo also has an account — no doubt drawn chiefly from Norse sources[1] — of the death of Balder. It differs materially from the narrative in the Eddas. In Saxo's story the name of Balder's slayer is Hother, son of Hothbrod. He is not a blind god, but a bold and well-favored prince who from his youth has distinguished himself for bodily strength and adroitness in all manly exercises. He has no equal as a swimmer and as a bowman, and no one can match him in playing the harp. He loves Nanna, the daughter of his foster father Gevar, and she returns his love. Odin's son, the mighty Balder, sees her and pays court to her; being disappointed in his suit, he seeks to kill Hother. From certain ForestMaidens Hother learns the entire plot; in consultation with his foster father Gevar he ascertains that the only means of wounding Balder is the sword of the Forest-Troll Miming. With much difficulty he gains possession of this sword. Balder makes war on Hother and Gevar, in the course of which he loses a great battle at sea, although all of the gods, even Odin and Thor, fight on his side; Thor crushes down with his cudgel all that oppose him until Hother succeeds in splitting the shaft of it; then even the gods take flight. Now Hother weds Nanna and becomes king of Sweden, which land is his domain by hereditary right. Balder continues the struggle against him, now with a greater measure of good fortune, gains the victory over him in two battles, and thus wins the kingdom of Denmark, which Hother has sought to lay under tribute to himself. But Balder's unhappy love for Nanna consumes his strength. No longer able to walk, he is compelled to ride in a chariot. In order to help him regain his vigor, three Celestial Maidens brew for him a drink made from the poison of serpents. Hother, meanwhile, gains knowledge of the posture of affairs from the same three Forest-Maidens who assisted him before, and makes opportune haste to join battle with Balder; the battle which ensues between them lasts a whole day, and neither side wins a decisive victory. During the night Hother sallies forth to meet the Maidens who are preparing the potent draught; he asks them to give him some of it, but they dare not heed his request, although they are well disposed toward him in all things else. On his return journey by a happy chance he encounters Balder alone. He wounds him with his sword, and Balder dies three days afterward. Hother now becomes king also in Denmark. Odin, meaning to avenge the death of Balder, seeks the advice of soothsayers, and the Finn Rostiophus tells him that Rind, daughter of the king of

Ruthenia (Russia) is to bear him a son who will avenge his brother. Assuming a disguise, Odin enters the service of the king as a soldier and performs such incredible deeds of valor that he becomes the king's most highly trusted henchman. Now he pays court to Rind with the consent of the king; but, too haughty to accept him, she sends him away with a box on the ear. The next year he returns in the guise of a smith and fashions for the princess the most lovely ornaments of gold and silver; but instead of the kiss he asks for, he gets only a second box on the ear, the princess being unwilling to favor a man so old. The third time he appears as the gayest of knights, but his courtship meets with no better luck than before. At last he returns in the likeness of a young girl, and so finds a place among Rind's handmaidens. The handmaiden, as he calls himself, pretends to unusual skill in healing. When the princess in the course of time falls ill of a dangerous malady, the handmaiden is summoned and, on being promised her love as a guerdon, restores Rind to health. Thus Odin gains what he has long sought. Rind becomes his consort and bears him a son, whom Saxo calls Bous and who is no doubt to be identified with the Vali of the Eddas. Of him Saxo relates only that he makes war on Hother, that Hother falls in battle, but that Bous receives a mortal wound from which he dies on the following day. The Eddas, on the other hand, represent Vali as still living, inasmuch as he is one of the small number of gods who are to survive the Twilight of the Gods.

CHAPTER FORTY-TWO

THE DEATH OF KVASIR — SUTTUNG

The death of Kvasir occasioned the dissemination among men of a knowledge of the poetic arts. It happened in the following manner:

Kvasir[1] was in the habit of journeying hither and thither in the world for the purpose of teaching wisdom to men. Once upon a time he was invited to visit the home of the Dwarfs Fjalar and Galar; they begged permission to speak a word or two with him in private, and promptly killed him. His blood they allowed to drip into two crocks and a kettle; then they mixed honey with the blood and from this pottage they brewed a mead possessing the peculiar virtue that whoever should drink of it would become a skald or a soothsayer. The two crocks are called Son and Bodn, and the kettle Odrœrir. The Dwarfs told the Æsir that Kvasir had been drowned in his own perfect wisdom, no man being wise enough to match wits with him. Some time later the Dwarfs invited into their home a Giant named Gilling and his wife. The Dwarfs asked the Giant to row out to sea to fish with them; as they were rowing along the shore, the boat struck a reef and overturned. Gilling, being unable to swim, was drowned, while the Dwarfs managed to right the boat and reach land. When they told the Giant's wife of the accident, she moaned and wept aloud. Fjalar suggested that it might ease her grief to look out to sea where her hushand had perished, and the thought pleased her; whereupon Fjalar directed his brother Galar to take a millstone, post himself above the door, and drop the stone on her head as she stepped out, for he was heartily wearied with her lamentations. Galar did as he was told. When Suttung, Gilling's son, learned what had happened, he came upon the Dwarfs, took them captive, and marooned them on a reef over which the sea washed at flood tide. In their distress they begged Suttung to have mercy on them and offered to give him the precious mead in recompense for his father's death. Suttung accepted their proffer, and in this way a reconciliation was effected between them. He hid the mead at a place called Nitbjorg and set his daughter Gunnlod to keep watch over it.

When all these events came to the knowledge of Odin, he set out determined to secure the mead for himself. In his journey he came to a meadow belonging to Suttung's brother Baugi, where he saw nine thralls at work cutting hay. On his asking if they wanted their scythes sharpened they gladly accepted his services. Taking his whetstone from his belt he put such a fine edge on the scythes that the thralls were eager to buy the whetstone from him. He was willing to sell, but finding that each one of them coveted it, he tossed the whetstone into the air; all of them tried to catch it at one time, and thus had the misfortune to cut one another's throats with their scythes. Now Odin found lodging for the night with Baugi. Baugi complained to Odin that his nine thralls had killed one another, and that he was at his wits' end to get laborers in their stead. Odin, who had called himself Bolverk, offered to do nine men's work for Baugi, if Baugi would only procure him a draught of Suttung's mead by way of wages. Baugi answered that, though he had no sort of control over the mead, which Suttung kept in his own charge alone, he was willing to go in the company of Bolverk and try to gain possession of the mead for him. While summer lasted, Bolverk did the work of nine men for Baugi; but when winter came, he demanded his hire. The two accordingly visited Suttung, to whom Baugi explained the agreement between himself and Bolverk; but Suttung refused outright to let them have so much as a single drop. Bolverk then proposed to Baugi that they would have to try to get hold of the mead by some sort of trickery, and Baugi was nothing loath. Bolverk produced an auger called Rati and asked Baugi to bore a hole with it through the mountain, that is, provided the auger would bite rock. Baugi set to work and had not bored a great while before he declared that he had made a hole clear through the stone of the mountain. On Bolverk's blowing into the hole, however, the grit flew back into his face; having thus discovered that Baugi meant to fool him, Bolverk enjoined him to bore again in sober earnest. Baugi plied the auger a second time; and when Bolverk blew once more, the dust flew inward. Bolverk now transformed himself into a snake and crawled through the hole. Baugi tried to pierce his body with the auger but failed. Odin soon made his way to the spot where Gunnlod sat guarding the mead, and remained there with her three nights. She gave him leave to drink thrice of the mead; the first time he drained Odrœrir, the second time Bodn, and the third time Son. Then taking on the form of an eagle, he flew away as fast as ever he could fly. When Suttung became aware of what was going on, he too assumed the shape of an eagle and spread his wings in pursuit of Odin. When the Æsir caught sight of Odin flying toward home, they placed their crocks out in the courtyard. On alighting within the walls of Asgard, Odin spewed the mead into the crocks; but Suttung having by that time nearly overtaken him, he let a part of the mead slip behind him. The gods, however, were not in the least disturbed, and permitted who would to gather up the dregs. Odin made a gift of the mead to the Æsir and to all who understand the art of poetry; the remnants of mead which fell into the mire became the allotted portion of poetasters.

CHAPTER FORTY-THREE

ODIN'S DEBATE WITH VAFTHRUDNIR

Just as Thor was accustomed to make adventurous sorties in order to discomfit the Giants with material weapons, so Odin from time to time undertook to match wits with them; to this end he would send out challenges inviting them to try their wisdom against his own. Among the Giants was an old wiseacre named Vafthrudnir, famous for his knowledge of the ancient history of the universe and of the gods themselves; with him Odin wished to debate for mastery. Frigg begged him to forgo his purpose on the plea that no one could compete with Vafthrudnir; but since Odin was determined, Frigg could do nothing else than wish him luck and express the hope that his wisdom would not be found wanting in the hour of trial. Odin accordingly sought out Vafthrudnir; presenting himself under the name of Gagnrad,[1] he let it be known that he had come to discover whether Vafthrudnir was really so wise as rumor had made him out to be. "You shall not escape from my hall," said Vafthrudnir, "if your wisdom does not surpass my own; meanwhile, take a seat and we shall see which of us two knows the more." Gagnrad, declining the proffered seat, declared that a poor man coming to a rich man's house should either speak sound sense or remain silent; if he let his words run wild, he courted certain misfortune. "Tell me, then, Gagnrad, since you choose to plead your cause from the floor," said Vafthrudnir — and he forthwith began to put questions about the horses of Night and Day, about the river Iving that forms the boundary between gods and Giants, and about the plains of Vigrid, where the battle between the gods and the Giants is destined to take place. Gagnrad made ready response to all these questions and then took a seat to propound his own queries. The one who suffered defeat was to lose his head. Gagnrad in his turn questioned Vafthrudnir about the making of the earth from Ymir's body, about the sun and moon, about day and night, about Ymir's or Aurgelmir's origin in the Elivagar, about Ræsvælg, about Njord, about the life of the Heroes in Valhalla, about which of gods and men were to survive the ruin of the universe, and about the passing of Odin. Vafthrudnir had an answer for every question. Finally Gagnrad asked what it was that Odin whispered in Balder's ear as Balder was being laid on the funeral pile. This question Vafthrudnir was at a loss to answer, and thus he understood that his opponent was none other than Odin himself. Then he confessed that with the mouth of one doomed to death had he bandied words with his guest; Odin after all remained the wisest of the wise.

CHAPTER FORTY-FOUR

ODIN (GRIMNIR) AND GEIRRED

On another occasion, too, Odin in person gave a great deal of information about the gods, their manner of life, and their dwellings. King Raudung had two sons, Agnar and Geirrœd. Once upon a time, when Agnar was ten years of age and Geirrœd was eight, they rowed off in a boat to catch fish. The wind drove them out to sea. In the darkness of the night their boat was splintered on the shore, and so they made their way to land. There they came across a peasant, with whom they remained throughout the winter. The wife adopted Agnar as a foster son and the husband adopted Geirrœd. The peasant couple were in fact none other than Odin and Frigg. When spring was come, the husband made the boys a present of a boat; and as he and his wife walked with them down to the shore, the man talked with Geirrœd in private. The boys found favoring winds and finally touched at their own father's boat landing. Geirrœd, who had taken his station at the prow, leaped on land; as he did so he pushed the boat back into the sea, calling out to his brother: "Go where the Trolls may get you!" The boat drifted out into the ocean, while

Geirrœd walked home and received a joyous welcome. Geirrœd's father had died in the meantime. Geirrœd was made king in his stead, and later became a famous man. Odin and Frigg were sitting one day in Lidskjalf looking out into the universe. "Do you see your foster son Agnar," asked Odin, "living yonder in a cavern with a Giantess and begetting children with her? My own foster son Geirrœd, meanwhile, rules over his lands as a king." "Yet he is so sparing of his food," answered Frigg, "that he stints his guests when he thinks that too many have come to him at one time." Odin declared that there could be no greater falsehood, and so they made a wager to decide the matter. Frigg sent her handmaiden Fulla to king Geirrœd with a message warning him to beware of a certain sorcerer who had found his way into the land, doubtless with the purpose of casting evil spells upon the king; the sorcerer might be easily identified because no dog, however savage, would attack him. It was indeed only idle talk that king Geirrœd was lacking in hospitality; nevertheless he gave commands to seize a man whom, as it proved, no dog would bite. The man, who was wrapped in a blue cloak, gave his name as Grimnir — in reality it was Odin himself disguised.[1] When they laid hands on him, he had little to say for himself, and therefore the king caused him to be tortured in order to loosen his tongue, by placing him between two fires and forcing him to remain there eight nights. King Geirrœd at the time had a son, ten years of age, who bore the name Agnar after his father's brother. Agnar, stepping up before Grimnir, gave him a drink from a well-filled horn, saying that his father did ill in torturing a man charged with no misdeed. Grimnir drained the horn to the lees, by which time the fire had come near enough to singe his cloak. Then he chanted a long lay, in the course of which he sang the praises of Agnar and reckoned up all of the thirteen dwellings of the gods: Thrudheim, Ydalir, Alfheim, Valaskjalf, Sœkkvabek, Gladsheim, Thrymheim, Breidablik, the Mounts of Heaven, Folkvang, Glitnir, Noatun, and Vidi, the home of Vidar. Furthermore he sang of the meat and drink of Valhalla, of the dimensions of Valhalla and Bilskirnir, of Heidrun, of Eikthyrnir, of the rivers in the realms of gods and men, of the horses of the gods, of Yggdrasil, of the Valkyries, of the horses of the sun and of the wolves that pursue them, and of the creation of the world. At last he recounted all of his own names and gave Geirrœd to understand that he had played the fool and that he had forfeited the favor of Odin. When Geirrœd heard that the man was Odin, he sprang up to help him away from the fire. The sword which had lain across his knees slipped from his hand with the point upward, and the king stumbled and fell forward upon the sword in such a way that it pierced him through the body; Odin at once disappeared from sight. Agnar, however, ruled many years as king over the land.

CHAPTER FORTY-FIVE

HARBARD AND THOR

Once upon a time when Thor had been away in the regions of the east carrying on his warfare with the Giants, he came on his homeward journey to a sound, on the other side of which stood the ferryman by his boat. Thor called to him, and the ferryman called out in turn, asking who it was that was waiting on the other shore. Thor answered: "If you will only ferry me across, you shall have food from the basket on my back; I ate herrings and oatcakes before starting on my journey and even now I am not at all hungry." The ferryman, who later disclosed that his name was Harbard, retorted with taunts, ridiculing Thor as a barefooted vagrant without breeches. "Bring your boat to this side," said Thor; "and tell me who owns it." "The owner is Hildolf the Wise, of Radseysund," answered Harbard; "he has just given me express commands not to ferry vagabonds and horse thieves across the water, but only honest folk that I myself know well; so tell me your name if you want to cross the sound." Thor told with great pride who he was — "Odin's son and Magni's father" — and threatened to make Harbard pay for his obstinacy if he did not bring the boat over at once. "No, I will stay here and wait for you," said Harbard; "and you will meet no man more difficult to deal with than myself, now that Rungnir is dead." "You see fit to remind me of Rungnir and his head of stone," answered Thor; "and yet he sank to earth under my blows. What were you doing while I did that work?" "I was a companion of Fjolvar five full winters on the island of Algrœn; there we sped the time in battle, cutting down warriors; we endured many hardships, but nevertheless we gained the love of seven sisters. Did you ever do the like, Thor?" "I slew Thjazi and tossed his eyes into the heavens," retorted Thor; "what do you say to that?" Harbard replied: "By artful practices I enticed the Dark-Riders to leave their husbands. Lebard, it seems to me, was a Giant hard to cope with; though he made me a gift of a magic wand, yet I played him false so that his wits forsook him." "An evil return for a good gift," said Thor. "One oak gains what is peeled from another; I each man looks to his own interest — but what else have you done, Thor?" "I invaded the east and there put to death Giantesses as they made their way to the mountains; great would be the progeny of the Giants if all of them were suffered to live, and small would be the number of men in Midgard. Is there anything else you have done, Harbard?" "I was in Valland and took my part in battle; I egged the heroes on but never reconciled one to another; to Odin belong the earls that fall in battle, and to Thor the thralls." "You would mete out unequal justice among the Æsir if it lay in your power to do so." "Thor has much strength but little courage; fearful as a coward you squeezed yourself into the glove, most unlike what Thor should be; you dared not make the slightest noise, afraid as you were that the Giant might hear you." "Harbard, dastard that you are!

I would kill you if I could only reach across the sound." "Why should you do so? You have no reason whatever. Have you done anything else worth mentioning?" "Once in the realms to the east, as I stood guard at the river (Iving?), the sons of Svarang sought my life; they hurled stones at me, but victory did not fall to their lot; they themselves had to sue for peace. What have you done?" "I too was in the east, and there trifled with a fair maiden who was not unwilling to pleasure me." "I took the life of Berserk women on the island of Læsey; they had left undone no evil deed, had bereft men of their senses by means of witchcraft." "Only a weakling, Thor, would take the lives of women." "She-wolves (werewolves) they were, not real women; they smashed my boat as it lay leaned against the shore; they threatened me with iron bands, and kneaded Thjalfi like dough. What were you doing meanwhile?" "I was among the armed men marching hither with flying standards to redden their spears in blood." "Perhaps it was you, then, who came and offered us most evil terms?" asked Thor. "I will offer you a recompense of arm rings, as many as they shall deem right who may choose to reconcile us to each other." "Who has taught you such biting words of scorn, the like of which I never have heard before?" "The ancient men who dwell in the mounds at home." "That is a fine name you give to the barrows of the dead. Yet," continued Thor, "your mocking will prove dearly bought if I wade across the sound; no wolf shall howl more hideously than you if I strike you but once with my hammer.

"Sif has a man visiting her, whom you may want to meet; prove your strength there, where your duty demands it." Thor said it was a shameless lie; but Harbard only crowed over having delayed Thor on his homeward journey, and

Thor had to own the justice of his taunts. "I should never have believed," said Harbard, "that a boatman would be able to hinder Asa-Thor in his travels." "I will give you a piece of advice, then: row the boat across, and let us bandy words no more." "Leave the sound if you choose; I will not ferry you over." "Show me the way, at any rate," begged Thor, "since you will not help me cross the water." "That is too small a favor to be denied," answered Harbard, "but it is a long way to go: first some paces to 'Stock' and then to 'Stone'; then take the first turning to the left until you reach Verland; there Fjorgyn will meet her son and show him the road to the land of Odin." "Can I finish the journey today?" "With toil and trouble you may reach your journey's end before the sun sinks, if I am not mistaken." "Our parleying might as well stop, since you do nothing but pick new quarrels; but you will pay for your stubbornness if we ever chance to meet again." "Go where the Trolls may get you!" said Harbard by way of a last word.

CHAPTER FORTY-SIX

RAGNAROK — THE TWILIGHT OF THE GODS

At last the time draws near when the existing universe must perish and the gods must succumb before higher powers. This period is called in the ancient myths the Dissolution or Destin? (*rok*) of the gods or rulers (*ragna*, genitive plural of *regin*); a later form is *ragnarøkkr*, the Darkness of the Gods. The gods themselves have foreknowledge of its coming, which is foreshadowed by many signs. Evil and violence increase. The Æsir's cock with the golden comb (Gullinkambi) crows to waken the Heroes of Odin's retinue; the dun cock in Hel's keeping crows likewise; so also crows the red cock Fjalar in the world of the Giants; and Garm bays vehemently outside the rocky fastness of Gnipa. For the space of three years the earth is filled with strife and wickedness; brother kills brother for gain's sake, and the son spares not his own father. Then come three other years, like one long winter; everywhere the snow drifts into heaps, the sun yields no warmth, and biting winds blow from all quarters. That winter is known as

Fimbul Winter (the Great Winter). The wolf Skoll swallows the sun, and Hati or Manigarm swallows the moon so that the heavens and the air are sprayed with blood. The stars are quenched. The earth and all the mountains tremble; trees are uprooted; all bonds are burst asunder. Both Loki and the Fenris Wolf shake off their shackles. The Midgard Serpent, seeking to reach dry land, swims with such turbulent force that the seas wash over their banks. Now the ship Naglfar once more floats on the flood. The ship is made from dead men's nails, and therefore the nails of all that die should be trimmed before their burial, to the end that Naglfar may be the sooner finished. Loki steers the ship, and the crews of Hell follow him. The Giant Rym comes out from the east, and with him all the Rime-Thursar. The Fenris Wolf rushes forth with gaping maw; his upper jaw touches the heavens, his nether jaw the earth; he would gape still more if there were more room. His eyes are lit with flame. The Midgard Serpent, keeping pace with the Wolf, spews venom over sky and sea. Amidst all the din and clamor the heavens are cleft open, and the Sons of Muspell ride forth from the south with Surt in the van, fires burning before him and behind him. His sword shines brighter than the sun. As they ride out over the bridge Bifrost, it breaks asunder beneath their feet. One and all, the Sons of Muspell, the Fenris Wolf, the Midgard Serpent, Loki, Rym, and all the Rime-Thursar direct their course toward the fields of Vigrid, which measure a hundred miles each way. The Sons of Muspell muster their hosts for battle, and the radiance of their levies gleams far and wide.

Meanwhile, on the part of the Æsir, Heimdal rises to his feet and sounds the Gjallar-Horn with all his might in order to rouse the gods. They meet in assembly and take counsel together. Odin rides to Mimir's Well to seek guidance there.

The ash Yggdrasil trembles, and all things in heaven and earth are seized with dread. Æsir and Heroes don their panoplies and march upon the fields of Vigrid. Foremost rides Odin, girt with his golden helmet and magnificent byrnie; brandishing his spear Gungnir, he presses on against the Fenris Wolf. At his side walks Thor; but as he soon finds himself in mortal conflict with the Midgard Serpent, he can give no aid to Odin. Frey joins battle with Surt, and Tyr with the dog Garm, who also has broken from his fetters. Heimdal fights against Loki.

Thor in the end kills the Midgard Serpent but is himself able to walk only nine steps after the struggle is over; then he sinks to the ground dead, borne down by the venom spewed over him by the Serpent. The Wolf swallows Odin, and so the god lives no more; but Vidar at once steps into the breach, thrusts one of his feet into the nether jaw of the Wolf, grasps the upper jaw with his hand, and thus tears open the Wolf's throat; his foot is shod with a heavy shoe made from all the slivers of leather that men have cut from their boots at the toe or the heel; consequently men should always cast such patches aside in order that they may serve the uses of the Æsir.[1] Frey falls at the hands of Surt, no longer having at his need the good blade he once gave to Skirnir. Tyr and Garm, and likewise Loki and Heimdal, kill each other.

Thereupon Surt hurls fire broadcast over the whole earth and all things perish. The wild, warlike order passes and a new life begins.

Out of the sea there rises a new earth, green and fair, whose fields bear their increase without the sowing of seed. The sun has borne a daughter as beautiful as herself, and the daughter now guides the course of the sun in her mother's stead. All evil is passed and gone. On the plains of Ida assemble those Æsir who did not fall in the last great battle: Vidar, Vali, and the sons of Thor — Modi and Magni. Thither resort also Balder and Hod, now returned out of Hell, and thither comes Hœnir out of Vanaheim. Once again the Æsir make their dwelling on the plains of Ida, where Asgard stood before; in the grass they find scattered the ancient gold chessmen of the gods, and thus they recall to memory the old days and speak together of the vanished past. Now that Thor's battles are done, Modi and Magni fall heir to Mjollnir. Nor are all among mankind dead. Lif and Lifthrasir have saved themselves from the fires of Surt at a place called Hoddmimir's Holt, where they find subsistence in the dews of the morning; from these two spring forth a new race of men. At Gimle stands a hall thatched with gold and brighter than the sun. There a righteous generation shall dwell, in joys that never end. "Then shall come from above the Mighty One, he who governs all things."

9 798886 843705